INDIGENOUS WOMEN'S REPRODUCTIVE TRADITIONS

Stephanie A. Sellers

INDIGENOUS WOMEN'S REPRODUCTIVE TRADITIONS

Reclaiming Sovereignty Through 500 Years of Colonization

Gender Studies
Collection Editors

Jan Etienne & Reham ElMorally

First published in 2025 by Lived Places Publishing

All rights reserved. No part of this publication may be reproduced, stored in a retrieval system, or transmitted in any form or by any means, electronic, mechanical, photocopying, recording, or otherwise, without prior permission in writing from the publisher.

No part of this book may be used or reproduced in any manner for the purpose of training artificial intelligence technologies or systems. In accordance with Article 4(3) of the Digital Single Market Directive 2019/790, Lived Places Publishing expressly reserves this work from the text and data mining exception.

The author and editors have made every effort to ensure the accuracy of the information contained in this publication but assume no responsibility for any errors, inaccuracies, inconsistencies, or omissions. Likewise, every effort has been made to contact copyright holders. If any copyright material has been reproduced unwittingly and without permission, the publisher will gladly receive information enabling them to rectify any error or omission in subsequent editions.

Copyright © 2025 Lived Places Publishing

British Library Cataloguing in Publication Data
A CIP record for this book is available from the British Library.

ISBN: 9781917503570 (pbk)
ISBN: 9781917503594 (ePDF)
ISBN: 9781917503587 (ePUB)

The right of Stephanie A. Sellers to be identified as the Author of this work has been asserted by them in accordance with the Copyright, Design and Patents Act 1988.

Cover design by Fiachra McCarthy
Book design by Rachel Trolove of Twin Trail Design
Typeset by Newgen Publishing, UK

Lived Places Publishing
P.O. Box 1845
47 Echo Avenue
Miller Place, NY 11764

www.livedplacespublishing.com

As an Indian woman I was free. I owned my home, my person, the work of my own hands, and my children could never forget me. I was better as an Indian woman than under white law.[1]

[W]omen are the base of the generations. Our reproductive power is sacred to us.[2]

—Katsi Cook, Mohawk Midwife, Environmentalist, and Activist

We're not feminists. We're the law.[3]

—Louise Herne, Mohawk Bear Clan Mother

Abstract

The work argues that the systemic control of female reproduction impacting Native American women specifically and the nations broadly is rooted in colonial and patriarchal ideologies brought to the United States by the European settlers. The examination of traditional practices and culture stories among Native nations, which includes coming-of-age ceremonies for girls, highlights the central role of female sanctity in the traditional cultural structures. Control of female reproduction has been a central mechanism for sustaining social hierarchies in the United States today, and this especially impacts Native nations where women and girls had, and often still have, much more latitude in their personal agency than those in western culture. The colonial ideologies were devastating to Native American nations that generally function(ed) from a more Gender Complementary social structure.

Key words

coming-of-age ceremonies, divine creatrixes, European colonization, female reproduction, Gender Complementary social structures, Native American women

Contents

Foreword by Jana McKeag	x
Learning objectives	xv
Introduction	1
Chapter 1 Since the beginning of time: Indigenous divine creatrixes and Gender Complementary civilizations	19
Chapter 2 Indigenous female sexuality, menstruation, reproduction, and motherhood	57
Chapter 3 What happened? How gendered colonial strategies targeted Indigenous women's bodily sovereignty and harmed the nations	81
Chapter 4 Stealing back the thunder: Indigenous communities decolonizing reproduction and motherhood	111
Chapter 5 Final thoughts	123
Notes	129
Recommended projects & discussion questions	139
Bibliography	140
About the author	149
Index	151

Foreword

Jana McKeag, citizen, Cherokee Nation of Oklahoma and president, Lowry Strategies Government Affairs

I have had the honor and privilege of teaching a class on "Contemporary Native American Issues" as part of Dr Stephanie Sellers's course on "Foundations of Native American Studies" for nine years. I was pleased to learn that my alma mater, Gettysburg College, had the foresight to include classes on diversity, including those that educate a primarily white student body about Native American culture and history that has for so long been ignored or, even worse, grossly misrepresented in our education system.

I am a proud citizen of the Cherokee Nation of Oklahoma and was certainly an anomaly when I attended Gettysburg College over 50 years ago. Since graduating from Gettysburg, I have dedicated my professional career to advocating for Native American issues, including serving as a lobbyist for the past 25 years. In that capacity, I have come to especially appreciate the work that Dr Sellers has been doing in educating her students about the horrors as well as the beauty of the story of Native American people in our country because those students will leave her classroom with more knowledge and empathy for Native Americans than the majority of congressmen, senators, and federal officials who I have worked with over the years. Those same legislators and officials, in large part, have failed miserably in upholding and maintaining treaties and the federal trust responsibility for the tribes that were entrusted to them decades ago.

I was especially pleased to learn that Dr Sellers's book would focus on the influence and importance of generations of Native American women, a topic that is overlooked and misunderstood. Like so many of my female Native American colleagues, I have been influenced and inspired not only by my grandmothers and aunties but by numerous Native American women who provided leadership to their tribal members as well as nationally in a variety of ways. Moreover, in the Native American tradition, which Dr Sellers addresses in her book, these women provided inspiration, wisdom, and leadership for generations of male tribal leaders.

My own story traces back to the Cherokee "Beloved Woman" Nanye'hi, also known by her English name, Nancy Ward. I am a direct descendant of one of the most famous leaders in Cherokee history. However, Nanye'hi was not influential as a tribal "chief" or "warrior". She was a diplomat and a businesswoman, and she was recognized for her talents by being elected as the only female voting member of the Cherokee council. Because of her talents, she was elected as the leader of the Cherokee delegation to negotiate with all male British and European American delegations, who were astonished that a woman would be entrusted with such important negotiations.

My more recent story, like many of the Native American women of my generation, goes back to my great-grandmother and my grandmother. Both strong, independent women, they divorced their abusive white husbands at a time when women did not get divorced. They were single mothers who, during the Dust Bowl and the Depression, raised children who went on to become attorneys, businessmen, and earn advanced degrees. When my great-grandmother's children were taken from her to attend Indian boarding school, most likely knowing that they may meet the horrible fate of other children attending the now infamous schools, she followed them to Haskell Boarding School, secured a job in the school's laundry, and stayed with them until they were able to graduate and leave.

After leaving her husband, my grandmother and her three children moved to Pawhuska where my grandmother, a secretarial school graduate, found work with the Bureau of Indian Affairs and Phillips Petroleum. However, she developed an ear infection and, because she was "Indian", she was prohibited from being treated at the "White" hospital and was forced to travel miles to the Indian Health Service (IHS) clinic. The IHS was infamous for employing doctors, nurses, and other medical professionals who, due to a variety of societal issues such as alcoholism and drug abuse, were prohibited from practicing medicine in "White" hospitals but were welcome in the "Indian" hospitals. After repeated trips, each time being told that "there's nothing wrong with you", my grandmother became completely deaf. Nevertheless, she was able to raise three children, all of whom graduated from college and became successful in their respective fields.

This is my story but, in Indian Country, it is not an unusual story. My female colleagues working not only in Washington, DC, but nationally on behalf of tribal issues have all been inspired, mentored, and motivated by grandmothers, aunties, and female tribal leaders. However, as Dr Sellers points out, it's not only the female advocates and leaders who are inspired by tribal women but the tribal men as well. My first boss, the brilliant Chuck Trimble, executive director of the National Congress of American Indians (NCAI), was the protégé of his fellow Oglala Sioux tribal member Helen Peterson, who founded the NCAI. Moreover, Mel Tonasket, the president of NCAI, was under the tutelage of another member of the Colville Tribe—the amazing anti-terminationist warrior Lucy Covington.

Both gentlemen provided leadership that has improved the lives of generations of Native Americans, but they could not have done it without the guidance of these remarkable women.

Although the book addresses the influence of these women in a historical and cultural context, the impact of their enduring generational influence is evident, and even growing, among today's Native American female leaders. You are probably familiar with many of them: U.S. Secretary of the Interior Deb Haaland, Congresswomen Sharice Davids and Mary Peltola, the late former Cherokee Nation Principal Chief Wilma Mankiller, former Mille Lacs Band Chief Melanie Benjamin, and former Crow Creek Tribal Chairwoman Sue Shaffer. Others may not be a household word but have been equally influential: Patricia Zell, Wendy Helgemo, Holly Cook Macarro, Sheila Morago, Valerie Spicer, Jackie Pata, Shelley Buck, and the like. Every tribe has benefited over decades from the strength and guidance of its female cultural, religious, and political leaders.

Dr Sellers's book is a tribute to a culture defining generations of Native American women *and* men. It is also the heretofore untold story of why and how Native people have endured despite countless attempts to eradicate their existence. And it is a lesson for future generations, both Native and non-Native.

Learning objectives

- Demonstrate how the creation stories of some Native American nations affect their social structures.
- Describe the impact of the divine creatrixes on beliefs about Native women and girls as related to reproduction.
- Contrast the beliefs about women in the American expression of western culture versus those held by some Native nations.
- Critically examine the beliefs about the roles of girls and women in society and discern their origins.

Introduction

Female reproduction is power: personal, cultural, societal, religious, and political. All human life comes through women and people who birth. We are the doorway between the realms of spirit and this three-dimensional world on Earth. Though adults of all gender identities rear children, females are the biological and psychospiritual hub—a term that highlights the interconnectedness of mental, emotional, and spiritual aspects of life, centered around female reproductive roles. We are arbiters of life. In many traditions globally, women gather the bones after death and conduct funeral rites. We are the original Alphas and Omegas of humanity. Ancient civilizations, as well as contemporary ones that still function on ancient beliefs, understand the profound realms of women across vastly diverse cultures. As the ancient Greeks recognized, a woman is "All that is"; as the Laguna Pueblo Indigenous people note, "In the beginning was Thought, and her name is Woman"; and in the Yoruba tradition of Nigeria, "Ajé is female power at all levels." Many historians, archaeologists, and anthropologists in western cultures have been working for centuries to ignore, discredit, and rewrite those stories of nations all over the globe that centralize femaleness, recognize female sanctity, support all forms of female reproduction, and bow to the power of mothers. To recognize how taboo and terrifying to patriarchy such a reality is, one needs to look no further than to the decades of vehement attacks by powerful gatekeepers in academia on distinguished archaeologist Marija Gimbutas (1921–1994). Gimbutas wrote volumes on archaeological evidence of the Divine Feminine in ancient European cultures and was blacklisted by women and men academics in her discipline for doing so. Gimbutas, a renowned archaeologist, faced significant backlash for her research on the Divine Feminine, which challenged male-dominated narratives within archaeology. Only recently[4] were those attempts at discrediting her research and claims about Mother-Goddess cultures magnificently vindicated, albeit posthumously.[5]

This book argues that the systemic control of female reproduction, rooted in colonial and patriarchal ideologies, has been a central mechanism for sustaining social hierarchies and continues to impact gender equity today. Female reproduction is fundamental to all aspects of human life, influencing cultural, social, and political spheres. Recognizing this allows us to understand its impact across many sectors. And what is yoked with biological reproduction, but sex and the menstrual cycle. So they too must be factored into the biological realities of human systems if one is to command the powers of reproduction specifically and the entire society broadly. Procreation is not merely a biological function however, but it reflects what cultures understand the categories of woman (femininity) and man (masculinity) to mean, the power those principles lack or assert, and who exactly has one, both, or fluid versions of them. Hence, from procreation comes power, but power for whom? And what do people who cannot biologically bear children do to gain the power afforded only to those females who create not only life biologically but who perpetuate culture by teaching its rules to the rising generations of human life? In addition, if reproduction is understood as sacrosanct and connected to the Divine, and you do not have that power, what gods will be created to position and thus exalt the non-childbearing biological sex and cast down those who can bear life? That conundrum was already addressed in geographic spaces overseas during the rise of patriarchy nearly 6,000 years before the European colonizers arrived on Turtle Island. In this new land to the colonizers, patriarchy had to be reasserted and institutionally standardized at all levels of society in order to undermine and control Native American nations, most especially disenfranchising Indigenous women.

The American Founding Fathers recognized the need for establishing a power structure that would assign people based on gender, class, and race `in their "proper" places in the hierarchy taking shape in the New World, and biological reproduction played a key role in that endeavor. William Penn wrote in 1681 that "[c]olonies are the seeds of nations...best for the increase in Humane Stock".[6] One of their primary goals in accomplishing that task was to shape social norms and laws about female sexuality and reproduction that essentially mandated serial pregnancies and forced motherhood for all women. Much of the female oppression rampant in the American colonies was imported entirely from English Common Law; thus, the Founders had little to alter on that score that mandated women and their children were the property of men. They did so to create a new government based on liberty and freedom—high-minded ideals in which Americans still take pride. However, those ideals had to be shaped by keeping the sexes in what they deemed their "natural" places: females in the home; males in government and commerce. The Founders looked to biblical edicts to populate the earth (with Christians) and connected fertility with patriotism. Ultimately, they looked through the wombs of women as one key route to make America exceptionally prosperous and an ideal model to eclipse the European nations from whence they came and, in many ways, disdained. Some of the goals from the nation's founding included not just American individualism and personal liberty but also ideals specifically related to reproduction, like "commanding men, domestic wives, and grateful, obedient children".[7] Reproduction in the colonial era was also a means to create child labor[8] to benefit individual working-class, poor, and enslaved families. To middle-class and wealthy families, having many children was a means for men to demonstrate social status and economic prosperity, as well as an expression of their perceived virility.

Promulgating the misconception that females have been subjugated by males since the beginning of time and that God has always been male anchors indisputable, universal male supremacy. These beliefs also assert that men are natural-born leaders. All these assumptions may have been easier for the American Founders to believe themselves and use to shape laws and norms if not for the Indigenous nations of the Eastern Woodlands. The European settlers were well-acquainted with the Haudenosaunee/Iroquois nations in upstate New York, the Mohegans of Connecticut, the Shawnee of Ohio and Missouri, and the Lenape in Pennsylvania and New Jersey, among many other Native nations in the East that functioned on matrilineal social structures. Whether by nation-to-nation negotiations or newspaper stories about lacrosse games and naming ceremonies or by the personal friendships and marriages between settlers and Indigenous peoples, the Founders and the population at large knew exactly what was going on in Indian Country in the eighteenth century: Native women directed their own lives within the cultural values of community, and their word was law to the nations. The Founders' letters in historical records unequivocally demonstrate their knowledge of these matters as well as their clear-eyed positions on female reproduction and the importance of controlling every aspect of it. This is how America was founded. Control of females broadly and reproduction specifically were critical lynchpins in the promulgation of the new American elite and the Founders' values, ideologies, and mythologies on what America could and should be.

For this reason, America continues its deeply contested struggles around female reproduction as some groups attempt to wrench themselves free of the oppressive past while others fight to sustain the original colonial norms that made females powerless in the eyes of the law. Putting those norms in context, we must remember that they were established by intellectually admirable men who believed in certain types of liberties. Some of these men also held a worldview that embraced the barbaric "appropriateness" of enslaving African and Indigenous people, militarily slaughtering Indigenous men, women, and children, and limiting all women's agency—essentially reducing us to our reproductive abilities. Though repugnant, accepting the paradox that individuals could uphold the concepts of liberty for some people and slavery for others at the same time is necessary to understand the founding of the United States. Rather than attempting to diminish the Founders' extraordinary vision and legacies to the U.S. on one hand or to ignore the atrocities they committed on the other are not useful approaches to a holistic rendering of U.S. history, in my assessment. Only when dismantling this reality by examining it through the lens of gender, race, and class—and connecting those concepts through a worldview of patriarchy—can we grasp how concepts can be twisted to justify and sustain our own privileges.

The apologists' claims that the Founders merely reflected the values of their era and thus should not be judged by contemporary ethical standards that value social equity is an academic misconception that utterly disregards the presence of social equity in Indigenous cultures that the colonists were fully aware of. Importantly, Indigenous peoples of the Eastern Woodlands certainly did invade other Native nations and take captives. There was at times political corruption in the nations along with every human ill that plagues us today. However, the widespread evils of race-based slavery, rape and domestic violence as commonplace, utter female subordination, and a brutal class system had no corollary in Native nations as they did in European countries and the United States at the time. Much of these forms of violence still exist in America today and are absurdly discussed as if they are normal patterns of humanity and not merely reflections of a warped cultural ethos! Cadwallader Colden (1688–1776), a governor of New York as well as a physician and scientist who was recognized as the best-informed man in the New World on the affairs of the British-American colonies, compared the Iroquois' governing structure to the [most admirable components of] the

Romans.'[9] Colden believed that the Indians in general, and the Iroquois specifically, "provided the new Americans with a window on their own antiquity [that] was shared by Franklin, Jefferson, and Thomas Paine, and a century later, by Karl Marx and Frederick Engels as well as the founders of modern feminism".[10] Colden wrote, "We are fond of searching into remote Antiquity to know the manners of our earliest progenitors; if I be not mistaken, the Indians are living images of them"—this was a belief held by many writers of this era, not solely Colden.[11] Last, Colden wrote of the Iroquois that "they allow no Kind of Superiority of one over another, and banish all Servitude from their Territories".[12]

My brief epistle is not meant to harshly admonish academics who so often ignore this history but to adduce that the social and governing structures of Native Americans in the East, and certainly elsewhere on Turtle Island, at Eurocolonial contact were generally egalitarian. What this means for reproductive agency is fundamental to that observation: since there were no oppressive systems of power in the East certainly that subjugated women socially and economically, there was also no regulation and oppression of them in regard to biological reproduction, marriage, and sexuality. The works of Native historians, anthropologists, professors, authors, and activists gathered in this book will demonstrate that position assuredly. Rayna Green addresses this issue in her review of ethnographic literature about Indigenous people over the twentieth century and notes the problems with western-cultural academic approaches to the study of Indigenous women in particular:

> The clichéd concerns that every discipline has with women—those primarily from their biological functions

as mothers, their social functioning as wives or lovers, and their economic functions as producers or helpmates—are still the concerns every discipline has with Native American women. Women as defective beings, psychologically, physically, or as inferior beings, socially, intellectually, and politically are yet the interpretive frameworks within which Native women are cast along with their non-Native American counterparts.[13]

Finding productive ways to reconceptualize the founding and creation of America, while including all the best attributes and worst offenses of our past, is imperative to move out of the American Dark Ages from where we seem at times to emerge but eventually slip back into its shadows in devastating ways, like the U.S. Supreme Court overturning of Roe v. Wade in June 2022. Female reproductive justice is the American litmus test of how far we've come in that endeavor. Considering news headlines in 2024, we are still grossly failing as pregnant American women in the midst of miscarrying are refused emergency medical treatment to save their lives, as their doctors are too frightened of being imprisoned to intervene.[14] Elected officials securing the highest political offices disdain women without biological children as "childless cat ladies" and claim that childless Americans are unpatriotic and have no stake in America's future.[15] This rhetoric echoes colonial-era ideologies that linked women's value solely to their reproductive roles. Honoring the contributions of our Founders, including American Founders of all genders, races, and classes who are rarely identified in that cohort, while simultaneously acknowledging their moral downfalls would be an act that signals American maturity. While we may love and admire our national "parents", we must also accept their tragic flaws that have negatively impacted our nation for centuries. Lying by omission about our robust and enigmatic histories in the United States, and burying profound collective wounds, only harms everyone and creates barriers to moving in healthier directions. Remembering the full American story is not an act of historic revenge or castigation of individuals or groups, but a form of reclamation that can only heal the collective.

In the Eastern Woodlands nations, Indigenous women not only ran their governments with complementary roles for males, but they also had wide latitude in sexuality and control of their reproduction. The Founders corresponded with one another about this issue that they dubbed the root of barbarous societies, namely, having women till soil they solely manage, express open sexuality, and limit their numbers of offspring. Thomas Jefferson wrote, "They [Native American women] raise fewer children than we do…The women very frequently attending the men in their parties of war and of hunting, child-bearing becomes extremely inconvenient to them…[and] it is said, therefore, that they have learnt the practice of procuring abortion by the use of some vegetable; and that it even extends to prevent conception for a considerable time after."[16] Further, there was anxiety among American elites that the agency of Indigenous women would influence Euro-American women to challenge their subjugated status. Indeed, that is precisely what happened, and the influence of Haudenosaunee (Iroquois) women on the feminist movement is well chronicled. The early suffragists had close relationships with Haudenosaunee women. For example, Mathilda Joslyn Gage (1826–1898) was adopted into the Mohawk nation as a relative, just as Cadwallader Colden had been in the previous century.[17] While some may argue that Indigenous gender complementarity is idealized, archaeological and anthropological evidence, alongside oral traditions, firmly supports the reality of these egalitarian structures.

Ensuring this part of American history remains hidden has been an ongoing problem in the full telling of how the United States was shaped in the past around reproductive restrictions, and how that issue is played out in contemporary times. We cannot know who we are as a nation, or why the war against female reproduction is raging as strongly as ever, until we look closely at the Founders' strategies and the presence of Indigenous women's sovereignty over their own bodies and lives. In the twenty-first century, we are still battling the legacy of the Founders' visions when it comes to female reproduction, as birth control and abortion are becoming more restricted and at times outlawed throughout the United States. In this way, the worst visions and intentions, not the best, of the Founding Fathers are still haunting America like starving ghosts who are invisible and unacknowledged, thus wielding considerable power over our country's psyche as we plummet into an era of wholesale, widespread anti-female attacks on reproduction. That means, fundamentally, attacks on all females' human dignity and agency and the ill health of our entire country.

From America's founding as a budding nation, it was profoundly shaped by attempts to control female reproduction: Indigenous women's, enslaved women's, and all classes of free women's sexuality and fertility were policed in the colonial states from points of desire to birth. The Founders focused on female sexuality and fertility to simultaneously further their vision of American exceptionalism in the areas of commerce, their versions of morality, and national governing. While Indigenous women's reproductive agency was undermined to dismantle matrilineal governance, enslaved African women's reproduction was commodified to sustain the economic interests of the elite. These divergent strategies illustrate the flexibility of patriarchal systems in maintaining control across racial and class divides. Since much of the spirit and language of the Haudenosaunee (Iroquois) Constitution ideologically impacted the Founding Fathers, particularly in writing the Articles of Confederation,[18] clearly delineating a system that ensured female subjugation was critical. The Haudenosaunee are governed communally by all genders with women central in that role. But Indigenous women of the Eastern Woodlands also presented the Founders with larger issues that were disruptions to the gendered power structures they put in place: Indigenous women had agency over their own lives. Attacks on Indigenous women—literal assaults and demonizing them through colonial writings—were necessary to upend their governing power. George Washington was known by the Haudenosaunee as "He Burns It" and "The Town Destroyer" for his campaigns against them. In addition, he especially endeavored to destroy the wampum writings that were not only the purview of the women but noted female controls of land. Jefferson wrote that those societies that allow women in the public sphere are barbarous and, in a letter to George Washington, made clear that women confined to domestic lives as wives and mothers allowed for a more civilized society and better governing.[19] The Founders' letters and writings reveal their anxiety about Indigenous women's reproductive agency and their efforts to impose Eurocentric patriarchal norms, a strategy that shaped early American governance.

Colonial-era use of birth control, abortifacient plants, spacing births to ensure proper childrearing, and so forth were standard practices among women, including Indigenous women, for centuries. What these social norms created in Native nations was female-bodied people's control over how many children they would birth, without stigma or repercussions. Reproduction was under the purview of Eastern Woodlands Native women as they had rights to the soil and the responsibility for feeding the populace through agriculture. When children are understood as identifying through their mother's clan—and not conceptualized as either legitimate or illegitimate based on male ownership as they were in Eurocolonial society—strict controls over the numbers of sexual partners and reproduction are unnecessary. To the power brokers of the colonial era, this set off alarm bells as imminent threats to the foundational values of the new nation they intended to build that privileged males. However for Native women, once the European settlers arrived with their patriarchal social structure that mandated compulsory heterosexuality that centralizes males and understood them as heads-of-households in civilized nations, this led to targeted attacks on their centuries-old practices. This thwarted their control over their reproduction as well as their sexual practices.

Punishments in the colonial era for unwed, free women who became pregnant included not only steep social stigma and ostracism but also criminal charges. In the 1700s, eight Euro-American women were hanged in the state of Pennsylvania for crimes related to "concealment", that is, hiding a pregnancy out of wedlock, which alluded to sexually transgressive behavior.[20] In fact, Mi'kmaq and Mohawk Elders note that for a 300-year period beginning in the 1600s, Indigenous nations in the Eastern Woodlands took in European settler girls who were pregnant out of wedlock. When their parents returned to retrieve their daughters, but not the illegitimate babies they had birthed, the Native peoples kept and raised the babies as their own.[21] Abortifacient medicines were widely sought after and sold on the open market—including advertisements found in Benjamin Franklin's newspaper, *The Pennsylvania Gazette*. From abundant sources, the power of female reproduction was central in the shaping of America and creating restrictions to ensure it would be expressed and understood in ways that privileged elite males was paramount in the eighteenth century, just as it is today.

For enslaved African women in the colonial era, there is a significant body of research that includes detailed data on how their bodies, sexuality, and reproduction were closely studied and regulated by Euro-American male plantation owners and physicians in the newly forming medical system in America. Gynecological records about these women provide abundant information about the Founding males' conceptualizations of them and the ways their agency was conscripted into colonial male controls. In the cases of both Indigenous women and enslaved African women, the American Founders were strongly focused on reproduction, but for very different outcomes. In the case of Indigenous women, increased childbirths that occurred from Native women's removal from leadership in their nations assured

Jefferson's and Washington's assertions that women belong in the domestic sphere to produce children. However, the increase in the number of enslaved African children meant an increase in resources for elite families. Hence, reproductive concepts and practices were selfishly shaped to profit elite American families, many of which continue to benefit from those legal statutes through their wealth and status to the present day. Though colonial proxies and political surrogates of the Founding Fathers of all genders who promulgate anti-female policies today still wage their ancestors' ideology of male domination, the fight against oppression has also not ebbed.

Connecting with ancient ancestral roots that come from cultures based on female sanctity is a critical part of the movement needed to transform global conversations away from "anti" and "pro" reproductive choice. Instead, approaches to centering women's reproduction in their own lives and communities, as it was done from the beginning, have more meaning and suggest long-lasting outcomes for reproductive health. Within those histories, stories, and cultural realities lie true emancipation from struggles women and people-who-birth wrangle today can find a deeper meaning about the power of our sexuality, menstruation, and reproduction. Most importantly, almost all cultures globally have stories and ancient practices that create positive meaning around women's biological processes, including reproduction. Seeing females as central in decisions about our own bodies is facilitated by reconnecting with those stories, just as Native American women were born to such a legacy in their nations long before the European settlers arrived.

Addressing the information gaps

There is a reason some stories remain purposely hidden. Some stories are delegitimized by cultural gatekeepers because the stories are not arcane, but dangerous to the elaborate mythologies about our histories we deeply identify ourselves with. When stories of dynamic gender equilibrium are built into a civilization's socioeconomic structures and shape its cosmology—yet coexist with a culture that subjugates women and exalts male supremacy—they are typically met with wholesale dismissal. When further brought to light, the stories are often suspiciously mocked because neither academics nor many lay people living in the gross inequities of a patriarchal social structure can entertain other ways of existing. This is why there remains a profound gap in American knowledge—including in K–12 and college-level curriculums about Indigenous cultures—when it comes to information about Native American gendered beliefs and practices.

Ethnocentric historic accounts and reporting on Indigenous nations of the Americas continue to distort much of the academic literature and research taught in higher education today, though significant inroads have been made over the past 50 years. Numerous monographs and volumes have been published that demonstrate a Red Pedagogy (Native-centered cultural points-of-view), and many are written by Indigenous historians, storytellers, researchers, and artists. These works expand on and correct fallacies in the historic and anthropological records concerning Indigenous histories and cultures. So, if the information is already in print, why has there not been more progress, more widespread recognition, particularly, of Indigenous women's agency and the Gender Complementary social structures of many Native American nations?

The answers are complex but are essentially that, despite archaeological and anthropological evidence, and the lived cultural expressions that demonstrate the indisputable reality of those cultures, most Americans (including academics specializing in colonial histories) either know nothing about them or utterly discount the existence of those Native gendered values. They often cite their reasons for dismissing Indigenous cultural knowledges as they stem from so-called poor-record keeping of Indigenous peoples—as if they had no historians. Some anthropologists' understanding of Indigenous oral tradition is also to blame for their invalidation of the existence of Indigenous Gender Complementary social structures, regardless of the availability of firsthand accounts, in print, in the historic records. Last, the presence of a divine creatrix and Native American women's agency and centrality in many of their nations are still at times discounted by academics as fantasies and utopian myths of Euro-American feminists or laughable fabrications of New Age spiritualists because such a cosmology in the Americas, or anywhere on the planet, seems difficult to accept.

Most significantly, the fact that American society today struggles to realize social and class equity, gender inclusion, dignity for all Americans, and a respectful relationship with Earth, while the civilizations that flourished on these lands before the European settlers arrived already had those components in their cultures—often constitutionally mandated!—highlights the profound failings of modern American culture. In addition, we appear even more disgraced as a country for the near-annihilation of those very people who were (and often still are) laudable models for human civilizations. Those pre-European colonization Indigenous civilizations included vast urban infrastructure, advanced mathematics and engineering to construct astronomical sites and sustainable urban centers, horticultural and agricultural development that fed populations in the millions, irrigation systems in arid lands, education, writing systems, sports, philosophy, and the arts—right here in the Americas.[22] My students are surprised to learn that some Indigenous Mounds in the United States were larger than the Egyptian pyramids,[23,24]—something they could have learned in middle school if only their teachers had known. Somehow, denial and amnesia—or *academentia* as my Indigenous mentors used to say—are still operative in the dissemination of American history as it relates to Native Americans. Since legitimate scholarship is based on evidence, and when the evidence is available for anyone to read, one must look deeper for reasons why omissions and misrepresentations of cultural facts persist. That is a key purpose of this book: to provide another source that speaks to the curricular silences around Indigenous women's reproduction, specifically, and the larger issue of acknowledging Gender Complementary social structures. Gathering more knowledgeable voices across all identities, and being committed to this work, is the way forward to support the flourishing of Native sovereign nations and a full-telling of American history. By reclaiming these narratives and centering Indigenous and feminist perspectives, this book aims to inspire transformative conversations about gender, power, and justice in both academic and grassroots spaces.

1
Since the beginning of time: Indigenous divine creatrixes and Gender Complementary civilizations

In the Beginning was Thought, and her name is Woman.[25]

—Paula Gunn Allen (Laguna Pueblo)

There is no other way for accounting for many of their [the Haudenosaunee/Iroquois nation's] institutions, and notably for that singular phase of society in which woman, by virtue of her functions as wife and mother, exercised an influence but little short of despotic, not only in the wigwam but also around the council fire.[26]

—1884 Report to the Peabody Museum by Euro-American anthropologist Lucien Carr

Any book about female reproduction must begin with the concepts of divinity and their impact on gendered practices embedded in the culture being studied. Cultural cosmologies lay the foundation for human beings to determine gendered beliefs about social and political power, personal agency, and definitions of morality that govern sexuality and partnerships, among most all other aspects of human life. This is evident because beliefs and practices shaping these categories of society are conveyed in a culture's origin stories. Indeed, how human cultures conceptualize the universe decides some of the most everyday matters affecting our daily lives.

While Indigenous cosmologies emphasized balance and cooperation, the arrival of European settlers brought with them a starkly different worldview that sought to impose strict hierarchies and control over female bodies, setting the stage for centuries of conflict. The gender that represents god in a culture is typically the one running the country. The answer also typically determines who is privileged in its religious, political, and social institutions. In other words, who in the culture can see themselves primarily reflected in the image of divinity and thus is afforded social power? Most power structures in cultures today are strongly grounded in gendered concepts from their religious origin stories regardless of their secular surface. Some patriarchal societies or segments of societies point directly and consciously to their religious origin story as proof positive of male supremacy and female subjugation, while others are influenced by these stories more subtly in the background of their so-called secular, mainstream culture.

European settlers' culture stories

In the cultures that emigrated from Europe and eventually created the United States, God is a single male deity who alone and omnipotently created life and the first human beings. The Paradise Myth, or Adam and Eve story, that is part of the origin story of the three monotheistic religions (Judaism, Christianity, Islam) that the European settlers brought with them, sets up gendered values that have been ascribed to all human females and males. Gender-fluid or gender ambiguous deities and people are not part of that story. These values have since been embedded in myriad cultural expressions in American society that profess male supremacy and female subordination, often in devastating ways. In the Paradise Myth, God says to the first woman, Eve, "I will greatly multiply thy sorrow and thy conception; in sorrow thou shalt bring forth children; and thy desire shall be to thy husband, and he shall rule over thee" (Genesis 3:16). Suffering in childbirth is by divine punishment. Wives submitting to husbands is the law. I am not offering a theological or literary analysis of this religious text but am pointing out the lived experiences of millions of people across time and geographic spaces who play out the messages of this story, unto today. Male headship of families and home spaces, even among nonreligious people, is still widespread in the United States. This extends to the "headship" of the American government and its institutions, even at times when women are at the helm, as they are expected to lead in patriarchal-defined ways that further domination rather than cooperation, individualism rather than the collective, and competition for resources rather than equitable sharing.

A vast body of misogynistic theological writings, philosophies, and laws spanning millennia lay the foundational concepts of woman and man in monotheistic religions today that impact secular law and social practices. To many clergy and their followers today, these writings are still operative in the functioning of their religious communities and are understood as being divinely inspired; thus these works are indisputable. For example, Thomas Aquinas, a still-revered influential Christian theologian and philosopher of the twelfth century, who was eventually sainted, asks in Question 92 of his *Summa Theologica*, "Should woman have been made in the original creation?" Though his question was certainly influenced by the milieu of misogyny in which he was raised and lived, it comes directly from the foundational shapers of western culture that also disdained women: (1) the theological tradition of St Augustine who believed women to be the "lesser" sex and necessarily subject to men; and (2) the philosophy of Aristotle who said of women, "a woman is a misbegotten man".[27]

Making a connection to how the creation myth of western culture that was brought to the Americas impacts legal and social values governing females is quite straightforward. The myth reinforces male dominance within families, upholds heteronormative values, and asserts control over female sexuality and reproduction as key aspects of a patriarchal society. Male primogeniture is a strong feature of patriarchal social structures that cannot function if the sexuality and reproduction of women are not controlled. Since names, goods, and social status are passed through the male line in a patriarchy, men must be certain of the genetic legitimacy of their offspring. To do so, the virginity of girls/women must be assured, and female sexual partnering must be reserved for marriage. Historically, punishments of social shaming and rejection for girls and women who did not follow these rules once ensured a lifetime of devastation for what would be called their "illegitimate or bastard" children who were also labeled and bore a stigma. This continues in many communities in the United States and abroad today. Moreover, while teen girls and women continue to face slut-shaming for having multiple sexual partners, the same behavior is often praised or normalized in teen boys and men. All these beliefs and punishments—stemming from a culture story nearly 6,000 years old—continue to persist in the United States to varying degrees and still deeply impact women and teen girls.[28]

Eurosettler culture stories in practice

Primogeniture and male supremacy require control of female sexuality and reproduction. The European settlers brought English Common Law with them to the colonies that galvanized biblical law into secular law through the writings of Judge Sir William Blackstone (1723–1780). He wrote that by divine right "a mother has no legal right or authority over her children" and also the legal statute regarding marriage: "The two shall become one and the one is the man."[29] In the colonies, women had no agency over their own earnings, children, or home. In the cases of intolerable conditions, wives had few recourses to secure their safety but to run away. Newspaper advertisements from the 1800s throughout the colonies featured notices from husbands reporting their wives' running away and publicly disavowing any financial responsibility for them.[30] These included descriptions of women that were similar to notifications for wanted fugitives!

In addition, the creation of pseudo-scientific theories and new violent practices enforcing controls over women arose in the 1800s in the United States. Social and religious controls were deemed inadequate to keep women under the control of fathers and husbands. More prima facie evidence had to be developed that appeared to be modern, biologically based, and medically objective. Accomplishing this would render such information as indisputable in the eyes of dissenters and, importantly, legally enforceable by newly minted physicians in the colonies who held authority in courts of law. These were the primary motivations for the rise, in the early 1800s, of American gynecology that was grounded in the exploitation of the reproductive powers of enslaved African and Irish immigrant women for the benefit of Euro-American elites. Practices springing from American gynecology were later applied to Euro-American women, like female castration (removal of the clitoris), ovariectomy, and hysterectomy, as they were understood as a means to treat so-called disorderly women, namely those who demanded equal rights, suffrage, and various social and legal protections. Women who simply disagreed with their husbands are included in this category. Punishments for colonial Euro-American women for voicing dissent against their husbands included dunking them in water and bridling their mouths with metal contraptions to prevent them from speaking. Public humiliation served not only as an intentional punishment but also as a cautionary message to other women and girls to remain submissive. These practices stem directly from beliefs outlined in the Paradise Myth where God rebukes Adam for "heeding the voice of thy wife" (Genesis 3:17). Early American gynecologists (circa 1860) "proclaimed that women are susceptible to hysteria, insanity, and criminal impulses by reason of their sexual organs".[31] Childbirth was another area where women's reproductive organs sustained tragic interventions by untrained, incompetent male physicians, according to a 1912 study by a Johns Hopkins professor. Despite this, the work of midwives was legally outlawed at this time, and male doctors' monopoly over childbirth sustained.[32] In 2024, American women still sustain the highest rates of childbirth mortality than any developed nation globally,[33] and the rates of unnecessary surgical births (Caesarean sections) in the United States are often attributed to those high mortality rates, among other outcomes that negatively impact childbearing and overall health of women.

At the same time that surgeries on women's reproductive and sexual organs in the United States were beginning, the rise of psychiatric controls was coming into vogue as well. The work of Sigmund Freud was imported to the United States and shaped concepts of females as inherently defective due to the absence of a penis, called "penis envy" (coined in 1908). Historically, American women who did not obey their husbands could be involuntarily committed to insane asylums by them.[34] The treatment of women at these institutions ranged from neglect and straight-jacketing to female castration—practices meant to silence and break their will. Diagnoses for women like "insane from childbirth, insane from abortion, domestic matters, suppressed menstruation, and nymphomania" were common reasons for being involuntarily committed, typically by husbands, to asylums, often for years.[35] Importantly, involuntarily committing Indigenous peoples to insane asylums was a Euro-American tool of colonization and persecution of non-compliant Native Americans. The Hiawatha Insane Asylum located in South Dakota was founded by Congressional legislation in 1898; this was shut down in 1934. A report from the Bureau of Indian Affairs acknowledges that most of those detained in this facility were not mentally ill, and that "nearly half of those confined there died from disease and deplorable conditions".[36]

Culture stories brought to the United States by Europeans set up the power structures based on gender that are still relevant and highly impact the ways that Americans understand, debate, and legislate issues around female reproduction. However, the imported, colonial culture stories setting up male supremacy and female subjugation had no mirror corollary among the Indigenous nations of Turtle Island (North America). On the contrary, culture stories among many Native American nations, particularly among the Eastern and Southwestern nations, strongly centralize female agency with women represented as their primary deities. Among most all Indigenous nations of North America, there was some form of gender balance built into their social structures that stem from their origin stories and, in many cases, those structures continue without interruption to this day. This was then directly translated into the lived experiences of Indigenous peoples from such culture stories, and Native American women typically had, and many still do have, these traditional roles in their nations today.

Non-Indigenous Mother Goddess cultures

Understanding the religious beliefs and histories as they relate to gender that the Pilgrims and other European colonists brought with them to North America is fundamental to understanding their impact on Indigenous nations presently. First, outside of North America, Goddess cultures flourished around the world for over 30,000 years.[37] Renowned scholars on this subject such as Marija Gimbutas and Joseph Campbell spent their careers researching and writing about the Divine Feminine and ancient cultures of Europe and the Middle East recognizing Mother Goddesses. Their works centralized archaeological findings of thousands of effigies of females as well as the literatures and myths honoring a divine woman in many cultures of these geographic spaces. Campbell wrote about the Divine Feminine's themes of "*initiation* into the mysteries of immanence experienced through time and space and the eternal; *transformation* of life and death; and the *energy consciousness* that informs and enlivens all life" (italics in the original).[38] These words describing the Divine Feminine are very similar to Paula Gunn Allen's description of the Indigenous divine creatrixes I will discuss later in this chapter. Importantly, neither Allen's nor Campbell's concepts are essentialist nor biologically reductive ideologies about women deities but are instead expansive definitions encompassing cosmological possibilities and power within constructs of female existence. The *j'accuse* of Indigenous and non-Indigenous scholars who write about Native female deities as being essentialist is a white-feminist understanding that is not culturally appropriate. Whereas biological processes are included in Divine Creatrix/Mother Goddess concepts, like the powers of menstruation and childbirth, they are not the sole nor entirety of beliefs in the preeminent power of women to create and be arbiters of life and death that supports whole communities.

In addition, recent claims in scholarship and journalism purporting that some of the thousands of ancient Mother Goddess effigies unearthed in Europe are actually pornographic images of women for heterosexual males have been debunked by ethical archaeologists. The original reporting, dubbed "Paleo-Porn", crossed into what might be legitimately assessed as not only absurd research findings but a pathologically biased gender interpretation that acts as an "an excuse to legitimize modern behaviour as having ancient roots".[39] From an Indigenous cultural point-of-view, this laughable interpretation is par for the course in the steady march of patriarchal research that can't seem to see beyond its own male-dominant world vision on every subject—and silences those who don't participate by attempting to destroy their careers. This trend has significant consequences beyond academic squabbles over history, however.

In a 2019 book-length study on the exclusion of women in contemporary medical research, author Emily Dwass deftly provides comprehensive accounts over the past century up to the year of the book's publication on how females are omitted and invisible in medical research, in devastating ways. In but one of many examples, Dwass reports how a medical doctor and researcher from the University of California shared that he was advised by senior medical colleagues that pursuing a line of inquiry about the role of sex in medical studies that moved beyond the sole study of male subjects was "a waste of time" and "could turn him into an academic pariah" because there was "no way attitudes and practices in medicine were going to change".[40] Considering the myopic cultural attitudes around gender and sex across all academic inquiries, it is no wonder there is so much resistance by even distinguished academics to entertain the existence of Indigenous divine creatrixes and the leadership roles of Native women in the Americas.

Continuing with the Mother Goddess cultures, Joseph Campbell writes that in "the earliest images around the fourth to third millennium B.C. ... [S]he is the overarching sky-goddess Nut, whose head and arms are at the western horizon, legs and feet at the eastern. Her spouse…is the Earth."[41] In addition, anthropologists observed thus:

> Nearly all [European] mythologies bear traces of the Triple Goddess as three Fates, rulers of the past, present, and future of Virgin, Mother, and Crone (or Creator, Preserver, and Destroyer). The female trinity assumed many different guises in western religion: the Norns or Weird Sisters of the north … the Zorya of the Slavs, the Morrigan of the Irish, the triple Guinevere or triple Brigit of the Briton.[42]

Around 3000 BCE, the Mother Goddess cultures began to decline, however, and the rise of patriarchal cultures in northern Africa, western Europe, the Near East, and India was observed.[43] The rise of patriarchal social structures and ideologies brought on by invading tribes created a historical and mythological shift in concepts around the Divine Feminine and thus the conceptualization and lives of human women and girls.[44] In these histories and literatures, "stories of female deities in the Goddess religion were replaced by the male divinities of the Indo-Europeans" and the "primary deity was changed from the Great Goddess, Mother of the Universe…to the Great God, Father of the Universe".[45] In practical terms, what this meant is that the Goddess Tiamat was changed to Marduk, Gaia to Uranos, Innana to Dumuzi, and that God/King/Priest replaced concepts, status, and practices of Goddess/Queen/Priestess.[46] Primogeniture began in geographic spaces and cultures that once were matrilineal and/or matrifocal, and women's mythological place of prominence was supplanted by her subjugation to men, as in Eve to Adam, Hera to Zeus, and Isis to Osiris.[47]

Also, the once-honored female menstrual rites became disallowed, and women themselves were conscripted to the role of original sin as impure and evil beings deserving of eternal punishment. Women's sexuality became a threat to primogeniture and had to be strictly controlled. Indeed, many stories arose during this takeover of the Goddess period, spanning millennia, that included the murder of symbols of the Goddess (the serpent/snake): Zeus kills the serpent sons of Gaia (Typhon and Python), Marduk murders his dragon mother Tiamat, Perseus decapitates the serpent-haired Gorgon Medusa, and Yahweh destroys the serpent monster Leviathan.[48] Even today, almost every statue of Mother Mary depicts Her standing on a snake representing the demise of so-called evil, which is actually a symbol of the Goddess. Patriarchal monogamous marriage was enforced as female sexuality outside those restrictions garnered ostracism, death, and women being labeled as whores and harlots, with their children deemed illegitimate and deprived of legal rights and status.[49]

Influence of European witchcraze on settlers

Another critical historical event that surely shaped the Pilgrims—and the worldview they enforced on Indigenous peoples affecting gender roles and conceptualizations of women and girls—was the witchcraze, or the European Women's Holocaust, that took place between circa 1400 and 1700s under both the Catholic and Protestant churches. Though data on exact numbers of women healers who were tortured and burned at the stake vary widely, the lowest numbers are in the tens of thousands, with the highest over 100,000. Data from the historic records include 600 women murdered in one year (or two a day) for certain German cities—with 900 murdered in a single year in Wertzberg—400 murdered in Toulouse, France, and in "1585 two villages were left with only one female inhabitant each."[50] The law "requiring the children who were said to have attended their mother to the Sabbat were merely [sic] flogged in front of the fire in which their parent was burning" was surely not only a warning to submit to church rule, but also to break a positive psychological identification in daughters with being female—an act that would have significant intergenerational impacts.[51]

The Pilgrims arrived on the Atlantic coast during this very era when the ruling classes of Europe were enacting a terror campaign against peasants and women leaders socially organizing against the rich and the churches. At this time, female sexuality was stringently denigrated and controlled. The phrase "When a woman thinks alone, she thinks evil" is from *The Malleus Maleficarum*, a book written by a priest in 1486 that advocated rape and torture of women persecuted for various crimes.[52] Also, lust felt by any gender was blamed on inherent female evil and fornication with the devil—themes one can see clearly in the Paradise Myth through the seduction of Eve by the snake.

This is the historical and mythological foundation that was imported to Turtle Island by the European settlers. The long roots of their religious history, particularly worship of the Mother Goddesses, were perhaps made deliberately invisible to them but were indisputably forbidden from being openly practiced even if they persisted in their cultural consciousness. The presence of female intergenerational trauma among settler women could be strongly argued as well. Nevertheless, the anti-female values were utterly operative in their religions, laws, and social customs—and utterly imposed on Indigenous women.

From the arrival of the Pilgrims and 500 years hence, the labeling of Indigenous peoples as demons, spiritually impure, and Native women specifically as sexually promiscuous and inherently violable is based on Christian exceptionalism that enforces ancient patriarchal beliefs about women and erases the existence of Two-Spirited (LGBTQIA+) people altogether. Further, portrayals of Indigenous men as blood-thirsty savages are also persistent tropes reinforced today by colonial sports mascots, the history pages of U.S. state governments that disregard Indigenous genocide,[53] and academic historic and anthropological sources meant to justify colonization.

Taking all this history into consideration, there is no Indigenous corollary to Euro-American widescale female oppression and, indeed, terrorization at all levels of the culture: from the origin stories to the functioning of households to social, economic, and political structures. Indigenous nations to greater and lesser degrees sought to balance gender roles because gender is a reflection of spiritual beliefs: the realities of Earth and Sky principles that make this world function properly. This is called a

Twinned or Gender Complementary social structure. Literary, cultural, and religious interrogations of Indigenous cultures must be grounded in that spiritual cosmological conceptualization in order to garner an understanding of gender and why there are clan mothers/chiefs, red chiefs/white chiefs, Beloved Women/male speakers, corn mothers/hunting fathers, and so forth. Though the Haudenosaunee/Iroquois nation's structure is different from the Navajo's social structures, which are yet again quite different from the Lakota's—as all the Native nations are quite culturally diverse from one another—there remains in all of them various levels of order and balance based in gender that are completely foreign to the western cultural mindset that sees hierarchies and pyramids in their understanding of economic leadership and governing.

Gender Complementary social structure

A Gender Complementary social structure is a framework where distinct roles for different genders coexist in balance; this ensures that no one gender dominates the other and reflects cosmological principles of balance. To understand a Gender Complementary social structure concept, one needs to begin by comprehending why Indigenous women's agency was specifically attacked by the Euro-American founders, and why female reproduction overall is still a mandatory target for control in order to maintain patriarchy. In a gender-balanced social structure, no gender has significant power to subjugate the other but, instead, they work collectively to ensure the effective running of the nation. By doing so, they are mirroring the balance of this planet through the earth and sky. Indigenous women's reproductive practices—indeed, the sum total of their social functioning certainly in the East—were targeted by Eurosettler founders historically because they had far greater agency than even their upper-class, privileged female Euro-American counterparts, which was a threat to white-male power.

Though a foundational position in academic feminist theory decries not only gender constructions for human beings overall, but gender roles in particular, as the sources of oppression, this perspective is incongruent to the power structures in Indigenous nations. Gender roles only oppress when there is rigidity in labels defined by external social institutions and when roles for one gender are understood as inferior to the other. Gender roles in and of themselves are not oppressive, just as gender itself is not oppressive; however, it is so only when values are placed on certain genders as inferior or superior to others. Indigenous nations demonstrate this reality in their practices, but many theorists have yet to regard these recorded, measurable, evidence-based cultural practices spanning centuries as legitimate voices. To do so would surely upend long-held academic perspectives and theoretical frameworks in Women and Gender Studies that often demonize gender labels and gender roles as the fundamental sources of gender bias.

A different perspective on gender binary

In addition, another contested term in today's feminist academic environment is "gender binary". Indigenous social structures and gender roles are often misconstrued through an ethnocentric interpretation of the term binary as a restrictive gender construction that is oppressive. This is not an appropriate, culture-specific understanding of Earth/Sky principles and reduces Indigenous cultures to simplistic interpretations of gender. Gender Complementary social structures that have gender roles for females and males are not fixed binaries that exclude individuals who by spirit or biology identify as something other than female or male—or whose biological sex does not match their gender identity. On the contrary, Earth/Sky principles (in nations that use these concepts) and correlating gender roles in the nations are fluid principles of dynamic equilibrium that recognize complex spiritual expressions in humanity and allow for individual expression of self. For non-Indigenous people, conceptualizing a world where there are no external institutions (dogmas, commandments, education systems, the State) dictating human identity and life controls but instead one that centers personal responsibility to the whole is quite difficult. Stories about Native people humorously mocking European settlers for their slavish obsession with group behavior (like submission to religious edicts, group conformity, reciting prayers in unison, living by a clock, etc.) can be found throughout the historic record. Gender Binary may be a relevant inquiry in western cultural academic discourse, but Indigenous cultures have entirely differing practices and concepts around gender. They also have many terms in their hundreds of languages that demonstrate their complex expressions of gender, whereas in American English we have very few.

Some Indigenous origin stories

Over the time we have been here, we have built cultural ways on and about this land. We have our own

> respected versions of how we came to be. These origin stories—that we emerged or fell from the sky or were brought forth—connect us to this land and establish our realities, our belief systems.[54]
>
> —Dr Henrietta Mann (Northern Cheyenne), Endowed Chair, Native American Studies Department, Montana State University

Creation stories of most Native American nations provide the traditional foundation for female agency in general, and reproductive practices specifically. Having knowledge of Native American divine creatrixes, twinned governing structures, and female sanctity is primary to understanding some of the experiences of Native women of the past and of today in terms of how these women from some nations regulate their biological reproduction. To be clear, the presence of an Indigenous female deity did not always translate directly to female headship of clans or governments, nor did it translate to Native women's cultural agency in monolithic ways across the nations even before Eurocolonial invasions—though in some Native nations it did and still does.

This section will provide a cultural background that created various worldviews about female agency that impacted reproduction in some Native American nations. In addition, it discusses how Mother Goddess-worshipping civilizations did exist globally and how the Divine Feminine ideologies are not unique to North America. I will also examine closely the creation stories of a few Indigenous nations and how those stories shape social and governing practices and, in many cases, female economic centrality. Recognizing that not all ancient human civilizations functioned from a belief in a single-male deity that subjugates females till today is critical for readers to understand how

U.S. control of female reproduction has everything to do with patriarchal worldviews and cosmology. Gender Complementary social structures were not just theories, perceptions, or cultural ideas, but were (and often still are) the lived experiences and socioeconomic and governing practices of many Indigenous nations of the Americas, as well as ancient Mother Goddess-worshipping cultures globally. How Native people have been subjected to the anti-female, religious-based, socially enforced beliefs of European settlers has profoundly shaped their reproductive practices and power as mothers from the eighteenth century until contemporary times.

Sky Woman of the Haudenosaunee and other Eastern Woodlands nations

> It is recorded in the Iroquois Constitution that 'Women shall be considered the progenitors of the Nation. They shall own the land and the soil.'…Native women are the sole, appropriate arbiters of land and identity…they can sense the land, for the land is a woman. It is, therefore, the Daughters of Mother Earth who make the best decisions regarding the children and the land of Mother Earth.[55]

One version of the Haudenosaunee/Iroquois creation story written by Mohawk author E. Pauline Johnson (1861–1913) immediately centralizes and recognizes female-headship. It begins with the line, "not taking her mother's counsel in the matter as she should have done"—on the matter of marriage—and introduces listeners to Sky Woman, the Woman Who Fell or Jumped from Sky World, who becomes the divine creatrix of Earth.[56] In this story, despite being married to a man, Sky Woman becomes pregnant from the Tree of Light when a beautiful blossom from the tree falls upon Her vulva "touching her with sweetness and a certain joy."[57] With tremendous strength, stamina, and courage, Sky Woman overcomes the significant hurdles presented by her wicked husband, as she eventually falls or leaps out of Her world down to the watery planet below. As She tumbles through the sky toward an unfinished Earth, white-winged birds catch Her. Then the animals of Earth, particularly the turtle, hold Her and cooperate in creating land and all the natural world. Much of Earth is created by Sky Woman's body itself. Seneca scholar Barbara Mann adds the next part of this story and writes that Sky Woman eventually births a daughter, the Fat-Faced Lynx and, together, they explore the beautiful Earth, plant seeds, invent new plants, and name all the animals and flora.[58]

So far in this story there are many profound teachings about what it means to be a girl and a woman. Heeding the advice of one's mother and the fact that the guidance of one's mother is primary to a girl are hallmarks of the story and any culture grounded in matrilineal values. Female sanctity and omnipotence are clear. Female sexuality is joyful. The female body is portrayed as strong and belonging to the woman herself—and not the property of her husband. Birthing a child that is not the biological child of a woman's husband is acceptable, even a nonissue. Matrilineal passing of knowledge is modeled. Strength, independence, and courage in a woman are lauded. The power to name, to invent, to plant, and to promulgate lies in the purview of the women. They do so without male participation and, in fact, there are no male humans on Earth at this point in the story.

In terms of the relationship with Earth, Sky Woman cocreates it with the animals who are already present on the planet. In this creation story, the animals are created before humanity and significantly participate in the creation of the biosphere. Therefore, human relationship with animals is established in terms of respect and kinship, forming a complex first family. This is an eternal teaching about the importance of human respect for the natural world and what a right relationship looks like between humans and non-human beings. Recognizing the sentient, intelligent, and spirit-filled existence of the natural world is not meant as a cute, primitive flourish to a fairy-tale story. Instead, it is an example of what is called intimate reciprocal relationships that is a teaching for a balanced life on earth. Indeed, the Haudenosaunee, as most Indigenous cultures of the Americas and beyond acknowledge and practice, recognized the awareness of all non-human beings and communicated with them, as some Native people still do. Reproducing this phenomenon in a lab or expecting to academically demonstrate these abilities are not fruitful engagements of what are understood as natural abilities of some people in most Native communities, particularly Elders and Medicine people. Gaining university researchers' approval and recognition are seldom valued as goals for traditional Native people who understand the complex workings of this world and don't expect non-Native people to grasp their advanced technologies of interspecies and human-to-spirit communication.

As the Fat-Faced Lynx grows into a woman, she is seduced by a spirit, becomes pregnant, and births twin boys. The Lynx dies in childbirth, however, and is the first human buried on Turtle

Island consecrating it as Mother Earth.[59] Before Sky Woman, now Grandmother, dies, she reaches into "her medicine pouch and flung the stars in the Sky creating the Milky Way...and She also lifted up the Moon so that her grandchildren might never be lost in time."[60] At this point on Earth, there are two females (Earth principle) and two males (Sky principle); two elders (Sky Woman and Fat-Faced Lynx) and two youths (the grandsons, named Sapling and Flint). From this arrangement, a Gender Complementary social structure is created that centralizes women and matrilineal identity. This narrative challenges patriarchal origin stories that center male figures, offering an alternative framework where women are creators and sustainers of life, thereby setting the foundation for gender equity in governance and community roles.

These teachings set up the Twinned Cosmology and cultural beliefs of the nations in the Haudenosaunee Confederacy that are found in the geographic spaces of upstate New York, parts of Canada, and Ohio. Their government is set up to balance earth/sky and female/male leaders. They have women's councils and men's councils that function somewhat as the American Congress and the Senate work together. Women as clan mothers are the complementary halves of men as chiefs. Gender-balanced structures allocate power evenly across all gender identities, and economic distribution follows a similar pattern as a "reciprocal exchange of goods and services".[61] With this method of "dynamic equilibrium",[62] the Haudenosaunee nation was, and still is, kept fully functioning in running its government and socioeconomic structures with a division of labor that was without oppression and marginalization of its people based on gender.

People who are now referred to as transgender or gender fluid would decide where they are going to sit (with women or men) to serve their nation, which was far more important than one's individual identity. Everyone's role in the nation was understood as valuable and necessary to its full functioning. Unlike in many nations today, what is understood as "women's work", like caring for children and a home, is often considered not only of less value than so-called men's work but by cultural standards is considered an affront to many men who are ridiculed for doing work beneath their status as males. Men's masculinity is policed when they engage in those activities. There was no corollary in the Eastern Woodlands where males typically, not in all nations however, moved in with their wife's clan upon marriage and played an important part in childrearing, especially in their role as uncle to their sister's children.

Iroquoian cultural practices that began millennia ago, originating in this creation story, continue to this day. Children are members of the mother's clan; women are responsible for agriculture, and work is completed under their direction. Women control their own personal property and do not lose it upon marriage. Also, women choose the chiefs and hold key political offices.[63] Last, and most importantly, male violence against women was historically not a widespread pattern or ideology in their culture. Colonial Euro-American suffragist Matilda Joslyn Gage wrote in the nineteenth century "that the woman of every Christian land fears to meet a man in a secluded place by day or night, is of itself sufficient proof of the low state of Christian morality".[64] Gage's friend Mary Elizabeth Beauchamp wrote that "it shows the remarkable security of living on an Indian Reservation, that a solitary woman can walk about for miles, at any hour of the day or night, in perfect safety".[65] Beauchamp's friend, a Miss Remington, who was a teacher at Onondaga (one of the Iroquoian nations), noted that she "often starts off, between eight and nine in the evening, lantern in one hand and alpenstick in the other...to walk for a mile or more. Without fear."[66] Additional evidence in the historical record of the cultural scourge of male-on-female sexual violence as standard practice among the colonists is demonstrated by Brigadier General James Clinton of the Continental Army who said to his soldiers in 1779: "Bad as the savages are, they never violate the chastity of any women, their prisoners."[67] William Apess, a Pequot minister writing in the early 1800s, demanded in his works: "Where, in the records of [so-called] Indian barbarity, can we point to a violated female?"[68] The absence of a cultural pattern of sexual violence against girls and women is another result of a Gender Complementary social structure and of female sanctity in their origin story that ensures everyone respects females; this is mirrored at all levels of their nation. This is not to suggest that the Eastern Woodlands were utopian, perfect, or without corruption. What is to be garnered is that widespread male-on-female violence, which is part of the everyday lives of Americans today either directly or indirectly, did not exist before the European colonization of North America.

Copper Woman of First Nations of the Pacific Northwest

From the Haudenosaunee of upstate New York to the First Nations of the Pacific Northwest, the valued roles of women in the nations' social structures are clear, despite their profound differences. Copper Woman of the Coastal Salish, Tsimshian, and Nuchatlaht First Nations in the Pacific Northwest is another divine creatrix who creates by using the fluids of her body and sets up a Gender Complementary cosmology grounded in the land and sea geographically housing those nations. In one ethnographic narrative transcribed by a Euro-Canadian informant and relative of the Nuchatlaht peoples on Vancouver Island, Copper Woman's story demonstrates the primacy of women's knowledge.[69] Copper Woman, who is created by a gender unspecified Creator, creates a male partner from her mucous, Snot Boy, and they have a daughter. Though Copper Woman is generative of her own accord, her male partner is a bit lacking. In this story, the beloved daughter of Copper Woman, Mowita, and her mother have a deep bond, and this bond is especially celebrated, highlighting the central role of women's lineage. In this origin story, there is also Qolus, a female, who turned into Mah Teg Yelah, the First Man, to be the husband of Copper Woman's daughter; this shows that gender transforming deities are part of the cosmology. There is also the Society of Women that "was intertribal, open to all women, regardless of age, social status, political status or wealth".[70] In that space, girls gained positive teachings about being female in body, spirit, and tribal responsibility. There is also the story of Tem Eyos Ki, a redeemer of women from the Waiting House (menstrual refuge), who teaches the forthcoming female generations about the sanctity of female sexuality as orgasm brings a glimpse of Old Woman (ancient women's knowledge). At the end of her life, Copper Woman sings, dances, and prays along the coastline sacred to these nations, returns to spirit, becomes Old Woman, turning her bones into a broom and a loom weaving the pattern of life and sweeping the shoreline.[71] Many nations in these Indigenous geographic spaces are historically matrilineal, though some had hereditary kinship balanced between mother and father. The Coast Salish people traditionally had Gender Complementary systems as they balanced a clear division of labor by sex. As in the story of Sky Woman, the story of Copper Woman sets in place the centrality of women and the primacy of the mother-daughter relationship as the source of identity for all people in the nation. Female agency is valued, as are the fluids of women's bodies. Two-Spirited identities are reflected in the story and thus LGBTQIA+ identifying people in the nation are acknowledged and have their sacred places in the community.

Changing Woman of the Diné (Navajo) nation

As a final example of an Indigenous divine creatrix, I note Changing Woman of the Navajo nation. Changing Woman was raised by First Woman and First Man to restore balance to the Navajo people during a time when monsters were destroying earth. She is a powerful, sacred deity who is "the source of familial relations, the clan system, fertility, and life power governing" of the Navajo people.[72] Revered deeply to this day as an integral part of Navajo culture, she sustains the current generations as they honor her through song, prayer, and ceremony.[73] Again, this culture story sets in place the value of females in determining identity in the nation, women's roles in governing, and female sanctity that has direct expression in everyday life.

Two-Spirit (LGBTQIA+) deities

Gender fluid, lesbian, and gay deities are strongly included, and often centralized, in Indigenous creation and traditional stories. There is the Navajo Mountain Man ("who looks like a woman but is a man"),[74] the Hwami of the Mohave ("the rare women leading men's lives"),[75] and Pohaha of the Tewa ("Even if she was a girl, she was a man, too").[76] Because of the clan systems and kinship networks of many Indigenous nations, a strict adherence to gender identity based on biological sex was generally not policed. Since clan membership was not based on heterosexual partners heading a nuclear family, LGBTQIA+ relatives typically fit seamlessly into clan families. As Cherokee Two-Spirit scholar Qwo-Li Driskill says of the Cherokee nation: "We were part of the circle." Also, communal responsibility is typically one of the highest values of most Indigenous nations—supporting and finding one's place in the collective, not individualism—rather than a system of external institutions (like commandments, dogmas, a police force) to enforce rules of gender normativity and heterosexual identity. Therefore, the agency of Native children in determining their sexual orientation and gender identity is well documented, along with the caveat that adults did not interfere with their choices. Understood not so much as personal choice or whim, as gender identity and sexual orientation are often presented in American culture today, but rather as fulfilling one's spiritual authenticity set in motion by the Creator is a typical traditional perspective.

What this means is that Two-Spirited people's contributions to the nation were expected to be similar to those of non-Two-Spirited individuals. Some of the duties Two-Spirited individuals particularly fulfilled in some Indigenous nations historically include the care of orphaned children and being medicine people (spiritual and plant healers); however, historic records note that some of them also demonstrate heroic military valor and cultural diplomacy. Driskill refers to the Cherokee term "asegi" (LGBTQ identifying people) as having multiple layered meanings to hir people—like an extraordinary other, a differing way of thinking and feeling, other hearted, and different spirit or possessing sacred roles. The complexity of these concepts alone indicates the spiritual and cultural power of those who hold a Third Space or a Third Gender in Native cultures. The Indigenous umbrella term for queer or LGBTQIA-identifying people, Two-Spirit, itself has been described by scholar Alicia Cox as a moveable shelter where Natives occupying that Third Space can find safety.

Other Indigenous divine creatrixes

In addition to Sky Woman, Changing Woman, Copper Woman, and Arrow Young Men (who were pregnant), there is Selu (First Woman and Corn Mother) of the Cherokee nation complemented by Kanati (First Man and Guardian of the Hunt). There is Spider Woman of the Hopi and Pueblo nations and Thought Woman of the Keres.[77] The Ojibwe honor the spiritual being Everlasting Standing Woman.[78] There is also Nokomis of the Ojibwe, White Buffalo Calf Woman of the Lakota, and Hard Beings Woman and Sand Altar Woman of the Hopi.

Both Nokomis and White Buffalo Calf Woman provide essential tools to Indigenous peoples to live well on Earth. Nokomis provide the tools to harvest the sacred wild rice. White Buffalo Calf Woman brought the sacred pipe to the northern Plains nations. Among these nations then, and many others, Indigenous peoples had women represented in respectful, powerful roles in their worldviews.

The issue of Indigenous matriarchies

Academic, anthropological declarations that there were no Indigenous matriarchies in North America demonstrate an ethnocentric interpretation of research that is ignorant of Indigenous Gender Complementary social and cosmological constructions and the central roles of Indigenous women leaders in many Native nations.[79] In their search for an Indigenous female leader who represents and governs in a manner similar to that of a patriarchal one, whose position sits at the pinnacle of governing power within a gender-dominating, hierarchal, class-based social structure in North America, they find none. From this, academics conclude there were no Indigenous matriarchies, meaning female-led governing and social structures. Their conclusions, however, are false. The denial of Indigenous matriarchies reflects a broader tendency in western academia to impose hierarchical, patriarchal frameworks onto Indigenous societies. This imposition not only erases the distinctiveness of Indigenous governance but also reinforces colonial narratives that delegitimize Indigenous knowledge systems.

The work of Peggy Reeves Sanday demonstrated years ago the existence of female headship of nations globally in her groundbreaking work *Women At the Center: Life in a Modern Matriarchy*.

But it is Indigenous scholars, like Paula Gunn Allen, Barbara Mann, Jennifer Denetdale, Denise Lajimodiere, and many others, who have written extensively on Native North American women's traditional leadership. Indigenous cultural anthropologist Kay Givens McGowan states unequivocally that the "great Native American civilizations of the Southeast of the present-day United States—importantly including the Cherokee, Choctaw, Chickasaw, Muscogee, and Seminole—were matriarchal societies".[80] Sto:Loh nation Elder Lee Maracle also refers to Indigenous nations of western Canada as matriarchies, adding that "the original economy was managed by women, the great sociological governesses of the past who held jurisdiction over the land, the wealth of families, [and] it was the uprooting of this matriarchal system that opened the door to inequity, shame, and violence in our world".[81] The problem for many academics is that they interpret matriarchy as a female system of patriarchy, so their obvious conclusion would be there are no matriarchies in North America, which would be correct by that definition. However, Allen's term "gynocracy", which entered academic conversations in the 1980s through *The Sacred Hoop*, defines a woman-centered and gender-balanced governing structure that was modeled in some Indigenous nations of the Americas. Though criticized, the term unequivocally stands valid after nearly 40 years of scrutiny and analysis and is cited as indisputable evidence in some contemporary Indigenous scholarship in Indigenous and Gender Studies. Cultural anthropologist Carol Markstrom cites this declaration in her book about Indigenous girls' coming-of-age ceremonies:

> Although the lives of Native American women differed greatly from tribe to tribe, their lifestyles exhibited a

great deal more independence and security than those of the European women who came to these shores. Indian women had individual freedom within tribal life that women in more 'advanced' societies were not to experience for several generations.[82]

In a sharp critique of anthropological and historical writings ignoring or misrepresenting Native American women's leadership in twentieth-century scholarship, Rayna Green notes "that no one has written about the modern female leadership in tribes that have been female-governed for a long time—Colville, Yavapai, Seminole, Puyallup, Menominee—or about the women who have been the political leaders of the last two decades, Lucy Covington, Ramona Bennett, Ada Deer, Annie Wauneka, and Pat McGee" and notes that unless approaches to scholarship changes "we will know less and less about Native American women".[83] A critical case in Green's point is the "Concluding Remarks" chapter written by contributors Daniel Maltz and JoAllyn Archambault of the 1994 volume *Gender and Power in Native North America* edited by Laura F. Klein and Lillian A. Ackerman. In this chapter, Maltz and Archambault directly attack Paula Gunn Allen claiming her work promulgates a "fantasy of an aboriginal matriarchy, a world in which women are the centers of the universe, controlling all power and resources" and that the Iroquois governing structure was "romanticized" by her.[84] This chapter as well as most of the edited volume completely omits the presence of a divine creatrix in most Indigenous nations and the important role they play in shaping worldviews as they relate to gender—which are then translated to social structures. But doing so would have centered the Native nations' own cosmologies, which would have radically changed their colonial, academic perspectives on Native people's cultures that, unfortunately, brim to overflowing in this often-quoted work.

Not Indigenous fertility cults

Another area of fallacy about Indigenous divine creatrixes is that they reflect the values and practices of not advanced civilizations where female sanctity was lauded and mirrored in the social structure, but, to the contrary, was a practice of primitive fertility cults. Understanding that a gynocratic social structure—one led by and centralizing women—could hardly be considered by most Euro-American historians and anthropologists (even contemporary ones!) as an advanced civilization is part of the movement that still categorizes Indigenous creatrixes as fertility goddesses of primitive people. A gynocracy is a woman-centered, gender-balanced governing structure that recognizes the centrality of women's contributions in all aspects of social, political, and spiritual life. As I noted in the Introduction to this book, whether archaeologists, anthropologists, or historians are researching ancient nations of the Americas, Europe, or the Middle East, the tendency is to do so with a patriarchal ethnocentrism that influences and miscolors the evidence of female sanctity before their very eyes. Turning almost every ancient European and Middle Eastern divine creatrix into a simple fertility mother-goddess is a fait accompli in the literatures and mythologies of many of those nations, despite the fact that the revival of their ancient status as powerful women deities continues within and outside academia. Quite often, archaeological findings and the words of Indigenous women themselves—noting female sanctity and women's equitable place in their current or ancient nations—are openly dismissed as feminists' fantasies and pseudo-academic research. Worse, academics have created concepts like "direct" and "indirect" sociopolitical power, and they attempt to place Native women of the past and present into these invented molds to better understand them. That's not possible when the concepts themselves reflect western cultural understandings of human relationships, not Native ones across hundreds of cultures.

Fertility cultism has various religious meanings, but when applied to Indigenous female Creators, this label suggests that women were once worshipped simply due to their ability to biologically reproduce—that female worth was reduced to their reproductive organs and breast milk. Thus, primitive people (who were ignorant of sexual reproduction) associated the maker of life/their god as a female, and human women as facsimiles of that female deity, because they had no knowledge of biology. Setting up a primitive versus civilized dynamic lays the foundation for the patriarchal belief that sophisticated, evolved societies recognize God as a male and as one who can create beyond biological reproduction. To most Indigenous nations, and civilizations the world over, this is an absurd conclusion since they can readily observe that biological males cannot reproduce and thus cannot conceivably be sole creators without the presence of a female. In addition, ancient menstrual blood rites of innumerable Indigenous nations around the globe ritualized women's cycles and their obvious movement and connections with lunar cycles, which rendered women not only as arbiters of life but also as "measurement/mother/originator" of the mysteries of the natural world.⁸⁵ In many Indigenous origin stories, the divine creatrix brings forth life without male involvement, which indicates, among a myriad of messages, that women embody complete potential and wholeness, creating from their entire beings, not merely through simplistic biological reproduction (if such complex biological processes can even be called simplistic!). Or, as the phrase goes, western cultural constructions of male religious omnipotence are clearly a case of "Venus envy".⁸⁶

Woman bears children, but that is only one part of her ability. As is directly espoused in the Haudenosaunee and many other Indigenous and creation stories worldwide, the power of life comes not only from Sky Woman's womb, but from her life-giving powers to seeds, to Earth, to naming, and all the creation She brings into existence. She is "the necessary precondition for material creation, and she, like all of her creation, is fundamentally female—potential and primary".⁸⁷ Reducing Indigenous divine creatrixes to fertility cults is not only a reductive construct of Indigenous cosmologies overall, but it demeans Indigenous women and their critical roles in leading their nations in the most practical everyday ways as well as in the most powerful spiritual ones. For example, in the Cherokee nation, the "head of the Council was the Beloved Woman of the Nation whose voice was considered that of the Great Spirit, speaking through her".⁸⁸ This is not a practice stemming from a primitive fertility cult, but one that lauds the power of women as a potent presence and arbiter of reciprocity between human life and the cosmos.

Last, in nations where female agency is modeled in the creation story—and girls and women are thus valued members at all levels of society—women's sexuality and reproduction are going to be under their own purview within the values of their particular nations. When a divine creatrix is sacred to a whole people, there opens the possibility that women and girls will also have full human status and agency over their bodies in that nation. The preponderance of evidence demonstrating that link will be discussed in the next chapter.

Summary

These are but a few representative creatrixes of Indigenous nations in North America. They reflect widely varying cultural constructions and expressions of linguistically distinct people, yet have a thread of similarity running through them in terms of sacred female representation in their cosmologies. They unequivocally assert in their culturally distinct ways that girls and women have sacred purposes in the workings of the universe and in everyday human life. They demonstrate female value in their own right, suggest some level of female agency in their own lives, and at times female leadership (in whatever way that might be expressed) in their nations. For example, as Navajo scholar Jennifer Nez Denetdale writes, "many Native and non-Native feminist scholars have pointed out that prior to Euro-American colonization, Native and Navajo women enjoyed a significant amount of respect and autonomy in their societies… gender roles were often egalitarian, meaning that both males and females were crucial to the survival and perpetuation of culture and society".[89] But that did not mean women were necessarily chiefs or held direct leadership roles in government, as Denetdale and many Indigenous women scholars have pointed out for decades. Equating the role of "chief" as the defining hierarchical role that Native women seldom held as "highest leader" is a western feminist construction that seldom translates directly to Native nations where women had, and still have, power as clan mothers or in other spiritual roles—power that is equal to or greater than men's power in the nation, even the chiefs. Therefore, avoiding oversimplification of how a leadership role is defined through a gendered lens in an Indigenous cultural context is critical before conclusions are made about Native women's power within their nations and over their own lives. Understanding these Indigenous frameworks of balance and equity is crucial in contemporary times, as they offer models for addressing systemic gender inequities and ecological crises. By acknowledging these narratives and the living nations that reflect them, we can challenge the dominance of patriarchal systems and envision more just and sustainable societies. As Cadwallader Colden and other Founders suggested centuries ago, if Americans want to know what a truly noble (i.e. equitable) society looks like, we need to gaze no farther than the Indigenous nations in our midst today. This observation remains true.

Indigenous cosmologies and gender roles challenge dominant feminist paradigms and offer alternative worldviews. For example, Indigenous Gender Complementary frameworks expand intersectional feminism by foregrounding communal responsibility and ecological interconnectedness. Liberal feminism is often framed as individual women seeking economic opportunity and equitable access to all social and political opportunities, whereas Indigenous feminisms strongly focus more on equity for the nation within the larger context of the United States. Centering the nation is a process of decolonization and protecting the land as a relative to the nation and the source of Indigenous cultural identity are key categories that Indigenous cosmologies support.

2
Indigenous female sexuality, menstruation, reproduction, and motherhood

> The women were the focal point of all [Iroquoian] social rules, with mother and mothers-in-law exercising unchallenged authority over the family. This social authority centered on fertility, childbearing, child rearing, sexuality, marriage, and divorce.[90]
>
> —Dr Barbara Mann (Bear Clan Seneca)

> [T]he rituals involved in the first menstruation represent a highly meaningful coming-of-age symbolizing a woman's power to give life that is first and foremost associated with the powers of the universe, and therefore linked to the rest of the community. Female rituals acknowledged the sacredness of life and the centrality of women's roles in society. [91]
>
> —Dr Brenda J. Child (Red Lake Ojibwe)

This chapter explores how rituals, reproductive practices, and communal family systems of Indigenous nations reflect deeply held values of Gender Complementarity and respect for female agency. By examining these traditions, we gain insight into the societal disruption caused by colonial patriarchy and the resilience of Indigenous women in preserving their autonomy. This chapter also discusses Indigenous female rituals and their societal roles in a few Indigenous nations of North America. Though they are at times broadly representative of the existence of menarche rituals in the hundreds of Native nations on Turtle Island, they should not be understood, at all, as representing all Indigenous nations because that could not be farther from the truth. Even in Native nations that have exceptionally balanced Gender Complementary social structures, the nations are highly varying and have distinct rituals for girls that manifest differently in their nations at adulthood. Gender Complementary social structures provide equity for all genders in governing the nation, in economics, and in society at large. Native nations in the contiguous United States had widely varying expressions of Gender Complementarity, including male-central structures. Though Indigenous nations do share many cultural values, like kinship networks and the sanctity of Mother Earth, they are linguistically, historically, and culturally distinct peoples with unique experiences of European colonization and contemporary struggles. To understand this notion, consider the nations of Europe: though they share some similarities in cultural values and language families, they also could not be more distinct from one another. First of all, they do not understand themselves as language families or culture groups, as anthropologists like to categorize Native Americans. Instead, Europeans understand themselves as Danes or French or Italians and so on. They take pride in their national identities and also in the sub-regions within those nations. This is also true for Native American nations that are distinct from one another and whose people take pride in their individual national identities. Therefore, a menarche ritual in one Native nation is going to look utterly different from that of another nation, though recognizing and respecting the transition of Native girls' first menstrual cycle marks a common thread among them all.

A way to read the discussion and examples I provide is to look at the larger patterns of female sanctity practiced in the sample of Indigenous cultures I note through their coming-of-age ceremonies and their control over their biological reproduction. In Eastern Woodlands and other Indigenous nations, the concept of motherhood is determined by the cycles of women's bodies, not necessarily heterosexual reproduction; this means adult women without children are still understood as having a role as a mother and are addressed with the honorific "mother" or "auntie". In some Indigenous nations, female sexuality had wide latitude, and the use of birth control and abortion were typically commonly practiced and neutral issues strictly under the purview of women and not under outside control by the nations. These practices were not only in the Eastern Woodlands nations, as is so often argued. For example, the Native American Women's Health Resource Center points out that "[t]he aboriginal people of the North Central Plains lived in not only a democracy, but also a matrilineal society…The Native women enjoyed a life unknown to white women in Europe, being free to own their own homes, participate in decisions about their government, and have control of their bodies."[92]

Indigenous women's menstrual cycles were often, and still are, understood in many nations as markers of important, even sacred, responsibilities in their nations' spiritual and governing leadership. Ceremonies still held in some Indigenous nations today, like the Kinaalda, Berry Fast, Waiting House, Ishna Ta Awi Cha Lowan, and so forth, were historically meant to honor a girl's first blood, and thus they provide irrefutable evidence of female value in the larger nation that certainly had a positive impact on women's self-perception and agency in their nations. This should not be interpreted as worshipping females but, rather, as including females as represented in sacred ways in the nation's cosmology that impacted not solely the everyday lives of Indigenous women but of everyone. Still further, the presence of menarche ceremonies does not mean there was absolute gender equality in those nations, by any means—socially, economically, or in governing.

What is evident in the traditional social structures of many Indigenous nations is that a far more Gender Complementary social structure was in place before colonization and that girls and women understood (and many still do) that their sex and bodily functions (like menstruation) were mirrored in divinity. That is a far cry from the stories the European settlers brought with them about Eve who bears the downfall of humanity on her shoulders and how that story impacted Native women, and all U.S. women, in our everyday lives. Resisting wholesale application of Gender Complementarity should not, however, be taken as an endorsement of inherent male dominance, which is precisely the assumption that has permeated much of the scholarship about

Indigenous divine creatrixes and girls' menstrual rites. Going to either extreme—whether discounting Indigenous gender complementarity or claiming the absurdity of utopian, matriarchal societies—does little to foster a nuanced understanding of complex cultural systems in place before colonization. Ultimately, having a divine creatrix and balanced gender roles seems to have positively impacted Indigenous women's control over their biological reproduction. Not having such models in western culture has certainly created legitimization, through the presumption of God's gender-biased divine order, in barring non-Native women from having similar controls as well.

Menarche and menstrual rituals

How females are taught to understand their menstrual cycles, the words their culture uses to describe it, and the ways their culture treats menstruating girls and women tell us much about the culture's level of respect for females as a whole, biologically and socially. Even in the twenty-first century, mainstream American culture and many cultures globally promulgate negative attitudes about menstruation that range from shaming girls and women to outright hostility to wage penalties in the workplace. Unlike the reverent treatment of menstruation in many Indigenous cultures, western societies have historically stigmatized these natural processes, as seen in phrases like the red curse, being on the rag, and associating menstruation with being dirty, bitchy, and equating it with female emotional hysteria—practices that are still common. In fact, significant work rewards are lost because of the needs of female bodies that create a lifelong subjugation "with costs to women's personal health and their careers".[93]

Throughout this chapter, the terms 'menarche rituals' and 'puberty rites' are used interchangeably to refer to ceremonies marking the transition to womanhood. The roots of these practices and beliefs about menstruation, which, of course, have changed in their expressions over centuries, were brought to North America with the European colonists. During the rise of patriarchy over centuries, menstrual rites were outlawed and the sacred associations of women's menstruation and sexual cycles with lunar cycles that governed planting, harvesting, and spiritual rites went underground. Of course, the human female menstrual cycle occurs every 29 ½ days, which is exactly the length of the moon's cycle, and monthly hormonal fluctuations, when in balance and spending time outdoors, flow to the same rhythm of increase and decrease with the moon's light.[94] The physiology of women's bodies expresses two feminine cycles: the monthly cycle of menstruation and the lifelong developmental cycle of menarche, pregnancy/birth/nursing, and menopause that all have correlations with the lunar cycles (new, full, and dark).[95] In ancient goddess-worshipping cultures of Europe, menstrual blood was venerated, and menstrual time was a period to reflect inwardly when women were understood to be "magical, mysterious, and powerful".[96] When worship of the Mother Goddess religions was slowly stifled and outlawed over millennia, more and more the sanctity of the female body was maligned. Again, the monotheistic religious stories provide direct prohibitions and denigration of women and menstruation in Leviticus 15:1: "The Lord said to Moses and Aaron…When a woman has a discharge of blood which is regular discharge from her body, she shall be in her impurity for seven days, and whoever touches her shall be unclean."[97] This passage continues at length noting various situations where women's bleeding—menstruation and postpartum bleeding—defiles everything she touches, including men. Again, women are associated with evil and the Devil in these religions, and churches in the Middle Ages forbade menstruating women to enter a church "lest she defile it with her filth".[98] The classic psychoanalytical study by Mary Esther Harding cites that "one of the reasons for women's menstrual disabilities and PMS today is that modern culture does not provide any kind of menstrual rituals" and that menstrual pain is not experienced in the ancient menstrual huts within community, but instead in isolation without "value or meaning".[99]

Rituals of recognizing and respecting menstruation do not exist as cultural practices in mainstream American society and in many cultures globally, although some individual families may hold an honoring ritual for their daughters at menarche. Such a ritual absence in American culture points to the lack of acknowledgment of female biological processes, at the very least, and, more importantly, the denial of spiritual and cultural meanings of female biological processes in ways that mirror the generative processes of life on earth. Indeed, not only are these menstrual rituals benignly absent, but for some girls, menarche is a confusing, secretive event in their lives that is meant to be hidden, particularly from males, which can induce feelings of shame.

Recognizing the power of these beliefs and social practices with which the European settlers colonized human systems in North America, their impacts on Native nations in regard to gender and reproductive practices cannot be overstated. Attempts to undermine the value, and in some nations the cultural centrality, of Indigenous women was not an antecedent to colonization, but a strategic endeavor to break Indigenous nations and people as a whole. Destroying Native menstrual practices and Native women's pride in their bodies, sexuality, and their connections to social roles were critical to attaining that fundamental colonial endeavor. I will address this further in Chapter 3.

Indigenous menstrual practices: A study of a few nations

Contrary to the misogynistic beliefs the European settlers brought with them to their so-called New World, Native American nations in the Eastern Woodlands did not have any cultural concepts or practices even remotely similar to the wholesale subjugation and marginalization of girls and women they witnessed in the European arrivals to their lands. As Onondaga Elder Jeanne Shenandoah writes,

> when we met these white women so long ago, I am sure that our women were probably shocked at the lack of human equality that these other women had to live under. And we, seeing them as equal—all women as equal—couldn't understand how not only women, but women and children, were living under this totally oppressive situation.[100]

Rituals and stories in a culture tell researchers so much about a people's gender values. The origin stories of western culture tell us how women and men relate to their male deity and present the conceptualizations and values placed on human females and males. The words used for female biological practices, and the absence of meaningful, widespread rituals demonstrating honor and respect for females, tell researchers plenty about western culture. So too do the rituals of the highly sophisticated Indigenous nations tell us about gender equity pre-colonization: a social value that twenty-first-century Americans, and nations the world over, are still profoundly struggling to achieve in our so-called sophisticated, advanced societies.

The Ojibwe Berry Fast

First, Indigenous people of the Ojibwe nation—who live in the geographic spaces now referred to as the American states of Wisconsin, Minnesota, Michigan, and North Dakota—traditionally had, and continue to have, puberty rituals for girls called a Berry Fast. Meanings from traditional stories "suggest that the power unique to females intensified and incorporated greater responsibility with the onset of puberty, when propriety was expected of young women entering a life stage recognized as sacred".[101] Ojibwe scholar Brenda Child goes on to note that "[e]ven very early observers of Ojibwe life noted that 'none of the subsisting Indian customs are more significant than those connected with the menstrual lodge'".[102]

Child explains that, for Ojibwe girls, menarche marked a time of mentoring by older female relatives who attended the girl's seclusion in a menstrual hut and imparted knowledge about her societal responsibilities. Traditional stories indicate that this period of seclusion and inner reflection during first menstruation also marked the time girls incurred spiritual power.[103] The hut could be constructed of spruce boughs, in one account, and the girls would abstain from eating for a period of days. After this period of contemplation, there was a communal feast, and the "preferred first food for the young woman being honored after the puberty fast" was strawberries that hold strong associations with the female gender until today.[104] This is where the term "Berry Fast" originated. The strawberry is of course a red berry, signifying the power of menstrual blood, and it is shaped like a heart and a womb. This red berry is sacred to nations throughout the Eastern Woodlands and has strong associations with female sanctity. Child notes that although female relatives largely guided this ritual, "male relatives and singers were sometimes present".[105] The puberty lodge could also be a source of receiving a sacred dream and a name for the girl, which would be spiritually empowering.[106] These rituals were not necessarily about fertility, but were more about the girl's responsibility as an adult woman, as it prepared her for taking on the duties required of a people who deeply value communal ethics. Communal ethics is a cultural value that acknowledges the value of all people, including the biosphere, and expresses responsibility to those entities through social norms and political policies. Therefore, the puberty lodge was not only about the girl's biological transition to womanhood and her spiritual guidance but was much about the future adult roles she would step into as a guide, leader, and mentor in the larger nation.

Child also notes that the entire year following the Berry Fast "was regarded as a special phase of an Ojibwe woman's life".[107] Some stories and historic accounts note how mothers guided daughters to be industrious and be "sensible and aware of her sexuality".[108] Overall, the emphasis of this puberty ritual was not about fertility or heterosexual marriage but was more about playing an essential and central role in one's community and being a responsible adult woman who realizes her body and spirit reflect the powers of the universe. Through the stamina and strength needed to complete the Berry Fast ritual (which involved fasting from food, enduring isolation, and respecting the functions of one's own body), Ojibwe girls developed the traits they would need to fulfill their roles as adult women within their nations. Contrary to western cultural expectations for girls, which emphasize culturally defined prettiness, submission to male authority, concealment of their menstruation, and expressing congeniality to all, Ojibwe girls are taught to be reflective and introspective, courageous and strong, and acknowledge their menstrual blood as a signifier of importance. This ceremony not only honors the individual girl but reinforces communal values of respect for female contributions, underscoring the importance of the interconnectedness of personal and societal well-being to the Ojibwe people.

The Navajo (Diné) Kinaalda

The Navajo coming-of-age ritual for a girl experiencing her first menstrual cycle is called a kinaalda. This sacred ceremony involves the community and incorporates the origin story of the divine creatrix, Changing Woman, into the four-day long ritual when the girl symbolically becomes Changing Woman herself.[109] Grinding corn on her knees, foregoing sleep, running daily, blessing her relatives, and getting stronger with the help of medicine people are some components of the demanding, complex ritual that is the kinaalda. At the beginning of the somewhat grueling ceremony, the kinaalda runs into the east to introduce herself to the Holy Beings. At the end of the ceremony during her final run, she calls out to notify the Spirits of her transformation into an adult woman. A key task of the ceremony is the ritual digging of a pit by the girl's male relatives and the baking of alkaan, a cake made of corn meal. In this way, the values of communal ethics are demonstrated and the girl is prepared through the ritual to step into a role to serve her people. Though the ceremony is for an individual girl to symbolically and literally transition from girlhood to womanhood, the larger purpose is for the community, the affirmation of Navajo cosmology and cultural continuance, and the recognition of the Navajo people fulfilling their role in the existence of life on earth. A key focus of the ceremony is on the kinaalda's strength, perseverance, and sacredness—attributes the nation lauds in girls and women. Most significantly, the Navajo girl represents the godhead/supreme deity of the nation, who is female, and is an emblem of outpouring Her strength to her community. This contrasts sharply with western cultural concepts of menstruating girls who are emblems of Eve's curse and the downfall of humanity, according to some interpretations of biblical scriptures.

The Lakota Ishna Ta Awi Cha Lowan ritual

Like the coming-of-age rituals I have just noted, the Lakota menarche ceremony, called Ishna Ta Awi Cha Lowan, prepares a girl for womanhood not only for herself but for her entire nation. In an even greater light, the renowned Lakota Elder Black Elk noted that the rites are for "the entire generation".[110] Like the Ojibwe Berry Fast, the Lakota girl is placed in seclusion and attended to by her female relatives. Regardless of the widespread variations across ethnographic accounts of this ceremony among the Lakota, Dakota, and Nakota nations that span centuries, there are a number of similarities in the rituals conducted for girls experiencing their first menstruation: "seclusion, special clothing and adornments, requirements of industry, instruction, and celebration".[111] Gifting of horses to the girl, organizing a ceremony called Throwing-the-Red Ball, carrying the girl from the menstrual hut to the tipi on a blanket, and feasting were also common practices. Some anthropologists note that in some traditions the initiate is bathed in water infused with sage.

This coming-of-age ritual originates with the deity White Buffalo Calf Woman, a revered being to the Lakota and other nations of the Plains. To these nations, First Woman was created before First Man and was "given power by the Spirit" and was "four-dimensional—all the Creation rolled into one human being".[112] First Woman was given a piece of flint by Creator, and thus she brought the first tool to humanity, much like Nokomis of the Ojibwe brought the tools for harvesting wild rice to the people. Later in the story, First Woman had Her moontime or menstrual cycle, and a drop of Her blood fell to earth. From this drop came Blood Clot Boy or the First Man.[113] As in the stories of Sky Woman and Copper Woman, the deities' bodily fluids created life—more specifically the First Man (like Snot Boy). This is an utter reversal of the Eve and Adam story where Eve is created from Adam's body. Though some non-Indigenous anthropologists discuss menstrual seclusion rites as cultural emblems of anti-female taboos thought to contaminate men's rites like hunting—or just men themselves!—the late Lakota Chief and Medicine man Leonard

Crow Dog addressed these so-called traditional taboos against menstruating women. In his teachings to his wife, the late Mary Brave Bird, she writes in her autobiographical work that "it is not that a woman during her 'moontime' is considered unclean, but she is looked upon as being 'too powerful'".[114] Crow Dog continues to explain that the old traditions understand women as having a strange force during their period that could undo the power of a healing ceremony, hence the restrictions in participating in ceremonies during their bleeding time.[115] Paula Gunn Allen asserts that "women who are at the peak of their fecundity are believed to possess power that throws male power totally out of kilter" and notes prohibitions on a Lakota yuwipi man (a spirit-filled leader) to stay away from a menstruating woman lest his powers be diminished.[116] Allen further points out that attempts to comprehend Indigenous menstrual prohibitions cannot come from "feudal and industrial people" as they will only see in their research rules imposed on women by men.[117] Instead, a legitimizing and Indigenous-centric point of view recognizes the necessity of many ceremonies in some nations that require the presence of a woman at some point in her cycle (menstruating, not menstruating, postmenopausal, etc.) to infuse the spiritual work with power. This is an utterly foreign concept in a western cultural context that comes with roots that reject out-of-hand female cycles as powerful.

The Lakota menarche ritual, like the Berry Fast, requires a period of isolation that helps cultivate courage in a young girl who most likely is experiencing solitude for the first time in her life. This teaching recognizes the value of female strength to the nation and, rather than admonishing female personal authority and agency as is done in American culture, Lakota girls learn that the trait is to be cultivated and openly expressed. The participation of the nation in the Red Ball game and the gifting of horses to the girl is a collective recognition of the important role girls and women play in their nation.

Indigenous marriages and family systems

In western culture, the concept of family in America once was strictly defined as being composed of a heterosexual couple with their own biological children and possibly additional biological relatives. This is called the nuclear family or the Standard North American Family (SNAF) that stigmatizes all other family structures.[118] With SNAF as the model structure, all other families are thus understood as deviant, and mothers are heavily marginalized in these families.[119] This narrow definition has expanded over the decades but is still broadly persistent in the culture and openly reinforced as the only legitimate family structure by some groups in the United States. This was, and still is, not the concept of family for Indigenous nations which, nearly across all nations, were constructed around clan systems. Seneca scholar Barbara Mann writes that the Iroquois longhouse kinsfolk were structured around the Mother-Daughter relationship and "[u]p to a hundred individuals might live in one longhouse, all of whom considered themselves members of the same large family…[and]…they felt inseparably connected with…all members of all longhouses of their clan, in every town throughout Iroquoia".[120] Family structures profoundly impact the meaning and role of female reproduction and its correlation to women's relationships with individual men and the larger nation.

Indigenous clans typically incorporated many people who were not necessarily biologically related but were connected by spiritual bonds. This remains true today. In more matrifocal nations, like the Haudenosaunee, men came to live with their wife's clan, and children's identities followed the line of their mother's. Though fatherhood was traditionally valued, proving male parentage, whether before or within marriage, it was not a necessity because a pregnant girl or woman had belonging, identity, and nurturance through her clan—as did her child. The child was not only hers but her clan's. Primogeniture was not a practice in more matrifocal nations, so establishing male parentage was not a relevant goal. Adults in the clan were part of the many parents who would help raise children. The role of the uncle in rearing his sister's children, or for any non-biologically related males in an important role in a child's life, is nearly universal among Indigenous nations. The father of a woman's children may or may not be her husband—a practice in place before colonization and certainly continued today—which was not deemed problematic to the Haudenosaunee or other matrifocal nations. Male ownership and validation of women's sexuality and procreation through heterosexual marriage were not values across many Native nations as the concept of the Virgin-Whore metaphor to characterize women's sexual behaviors generally did not exist until colonization and Christianity were brought to North America. The metaphor itself is entirely hinged on heterosexual male definitions and relationships to either elevate women for their complicity and submission (the Virgin) or condemn them for even perceived promiscuity outside male-defined parameters (the Whore).

In a clan system that is founded on spiritual relatedness, not biological ties, highly diverse gender expressions, sexualities, and adult relationships can find a home. In many cases, any adult woman is going to be understood as a mother, not only those females who have biologically reproduced. Menstruating adult women serve in roles as mothers, which does not narrowly mean a source of childcare! The concept of "Mothers of the nations" means Native women who lead, who govern, who are decision-makers in politics and law, particularly in the Haudenosaunee and Cherokee nations, among many others. Note that it is the woman's biological functions, her age, and her role and standing in the nation that makes her a mother—not simply having a child. Consequently, what makes Indigenous women grandmothers is the cessation of menstruation and reaching a certain age that garners respect. The honorific grandmother again is not tied to one's biological children reproducing their own biological children. This narrow definition from western culture is strictly bound to biology and largely by heterosexual relationships, notwithstanding modern medicine practices of in vitro fertilization and artificial insemination from a sperm bank. Hence, women in their own bodily autonomy and own seasons of their lives determine motherhood and grandmotherhood, not biological reproduction.

In addition, gender fluid individuals (including biological males) who identify as women will also be mothers, as the clan system provides room for any adult to parent. Therefore, defining the concept of family in terms of Indigenous clans not only disallows strict controls over female sexuality and reproduction, but it also allows for the inclusion of all sexualities and gender identities in the larger clan family. LGBTQ-identifying adult relatives have the opportunity, if not perhaps what could be understood as a "natural" or expected adult duty, to parent children—this means any children, not merely those who may be biologically related to them. Thinking of a clan as a group of spiritually and biologically bonded adults raising their mutual children communally, it is easier to understand how lesbian, gay, and gender-fluid people naturally belonged.

Marriages in many Native nations could be dissolved by divorce. In those cases, Native women had their clan to rely on for support, childrearing, sustenance, and stability. Placing a husband's belongings outside the longhouse for him to gather and return to his mother's clan was a Haudenosaunee practice indicating divorce.[121] Child custody did not exist in matrifocal nations as children belonged to their mother's clan and remained with them. In less matrifocal nations, children still had continuity provided by their parent's clan—whether this is their mother's or father's. In light of that stability, the fear of pregnancy outside of marriage—which plagued the Euro-American women colonists as it led not only to social shaming and shunning but in some cases legal punishments that included hanging (as I discussed in the Introduction)—did not impact Native women. In Native nations, there were no so-called illegitimate children or children without a name, meaning without a father's name, because children belonged to a clan, to a system of many mothers and fathers, many aunties and uncles. What this ultimately meant was that Indigenous children were surrounded by and raised by love.

Indigenous women's sexuality and reproduction before colonization

The Virgin-Whore metaphor meant to conceptualize and control the sexuality of girls and women did not exist in North America until the European settlers arrived. In many nations, neither did strict female sexual prohibitions and shaming. Though social expectations for Native women's sexuality varied across the nations, with clan structures universally practiced (in unique ways) that welcomed all children—not just children conceived by married couples—sexual relationships for Native women would be quite different from those under patriarchy. The obvious reason is that the goal of patriarchal female sexual control is the control of biological reproduction, and Indigenous nations did not have patriarchies, even in the more male-centric, male-dominant nations. Indigenous women across the nations traditionally had their own agency in sexual expression, and in matrifocal and gynocratic structures, female sexuality had wide latitude. For example, Cherokee women and men historically had highly erotic traditions and lifeways, according to Cherokee researchers like Qwo-Li Driskill, who discusses this in hir co-edited volume *Queer Indigenous Studies* (2011). In the work, an informant notes a Cherokee pipe bowl in the Harvard University Peabody Museum's holdings "with a man and woman having sex, in explicit detail, with their genitalia pointed right at the smoker. So, somebody's getting a little thrill looking at that".[122] European observers noted Iroquoian women's open sexuality and low fertility rates (due to birth control practices), like Father Gabriel Sagard (early 1600s), Joseph-Francois Lafitau (early 1700s), and

Thomas Jefferson (late 1700s).[123] Writing candidly, Barbara Mann notes, "Colonists noticed early on that, for all the sex going on, Iroquoian women seemed to cheat nature out of the frequent pregnancies experienced by European women."[124]

Reproductive autonomy and birth control practices

Native American women used various forms of birth control to space out and limit pregnancies. Thomas Jefferson wrote quite a bit about the low birth rates of Iroquoian women, as did other European chroniclers mentioned above. Jefferson noted that "[t]hey [Iroquoian women] raise fewer children than we do… [and] it is said, therefore, that they have learnt the practice of procuring abortion by the use of some vegetable; and that it even extends to prevent conception for a considerable time after".[125] Though Jefferson applied incorrect assumptions about the reasons for Iroquoian women's use of birth control, the practice stands irrefutably in the historic record and was obviously widely known throughout the colonies. Native American women were proficient in use of birth control methods to prevent conception, and some of those methods include "crushed roots of the red cedar and juniper plants in a tea…the boiled roots of dogbane or wild ginger, beverages made from roots of thistle, squaw root, and the Mexican wild yam…[and] plants to induce abortions and cause sterility".[126] In 1703, the French officer Lahontan recorded of the Iroquoian nation that "Native women drank 'the Juice of certain Roots' to prevent conception and to abort pregnancies."[127] The Chippewa also made use of birth control and abortion. As Elders today note, Chippewa women had medicines for unwanted pregnancies. Also, as was readily evidenced, "Indian families had only two or three children whereas white [colonial] families had thirteen or fourteen."[128] And despite all the assertions by non-Indigenous historians that there is little information about Indigenous reproductive healthcare during colonial times, historian Sylvia D. Hoffert writes in her study about the Trans-Mississippi frontier from 1830 to 1900 that "Native American women used herbs, plants, and medicines to prevent pregnancy."[129] These practices exemplify Indigenous women's deep knowledge of their bodies and ecosystems, reflecting a worldview where reproduction is a personal and communal responsibility rather than a tool for patriarchal control.

Seneca scholar Arthur Parker has documented how Iroquoian women's control of life had always been their legal right that included determining how many children they would bear—this was "entirely in the hands of women".[130] For Indigenous women—and for all people today—having control over biological reproduction has been, and remains, essential to prevent overpopulation and to safeguard sufficient food and resources for the nation. Further, child welfare and healthy development were priorities as well, so spacing births was valued. Doing so created a welcoming and nourishing environment for the children already born who would receive the attention and time from adults for sound emotional and psychological health. Iroquoian women spaced out and limited births to three to four children in their lifetimes,[131] which is a stunning departure from many colonial women who bore 15 or more children, and had many more pregnancies in their lifetimes, a burden that often led them to an early grave. In the colonial era, one in eight births resulted in the death of the mother.[132] Colonial women who were married "gave birth roughly every eighteen months or two years from their late teens or early twenties until menopause".[133]

Barbara Mann writes, "Most appalling to European observers was Iroquoian women's absolute control over their own bodies, and in particular, their right to choose when, if, and with whom they bore children."[134] Some birth control practices Indigenous women used were herbal preparations to prevent pregnancy, breastfeeding to space out births, careful monitoring of their fertility cycle, and abortifacients to bring on menstrual bleeding. Some abortifacient plants used by Native women in the Eastern Woodlands include the bark of the American Beech and the Prickly Ash trees as well as the Redroot plant for late-term abortions.[135] Mohawk Elder Ceceilia Mitchell states emphatically that women used abortion "when they wanted to", which is corroborated by Iroquoian tradition, law, and history; twentieth-century Cayuga Faithkeeper Chief Jake Thomas and nineteenth-century Cayuga physician, Dr Peter Wilson also validate this observation.[136] Along with plant use for birth control, Iroquoian women could refuse sex with their husbands,[137] which is still a fraught issue for many women married to men in the twenty-first century, as it was in the colonial era. In addition, the Ojibwe pharmacopeia for female reproductive health included "plants to treat menstrual discomforts, pregnancy and childbirth issues, and menopause".[138] Andrea Smith rightly asserts that "women have always had means of controlling reproduction… Ironically, colonial powers often tried to stamp out traditional means of birth control to ensure a large supply of cheap labor and a captive market for their finished goods".[139]

The Native American Women's Health Education Resource Center writes thus:

> Within traditional societies and languages, there is no word that equals abortion. The word itself is very harsh and impersonal. When speaking to traditional Elders knowledgeable about reproductive health matters, repeatedly they would refer to a woman knowing which herbs and methods to use "to make her period come". This was seen as a woman taking care of herself and doing what was necessary.[140]

Last, in a 2014 article in the news outlet *Indian Country Today*, staff writer Christina Rose cites Erin Marie Konsmo, Project Coordinator for Native Youth Sexual Health Network, on the topic of birth control and abortion among Native nations, noting that family planning has "always been included" in the communities. Konsmo outlines her organization's goals by adding that "[t]here were practices in response to our realities. If we didn't have food to provide for a large family or it was winter or we had to travel, a pregnancy might be terminated. In many of our nations, there still exists [I]ndigenous knowledge that would allow us to terminate a pregnancy."[141]

Summary

When a civilization is predicated on the individual rights of its people within a framework of communal ethics and Gender Complementarity, the obvious result is control over biological reproduction for the sex who menstruates, gets pregnant, births, and nourishes the young because oppression of them is not only socially unnecessary but is a violation of their worldview. Adding the existence of their origin stories centralizing women to these cultural practices that shape governing and socioeconomics only solidifies the position of Indigenous women as agents in their own lives as they hold critical roles in their communities for furthering the existence of their people. The Native Youth Sexual Health Network serves as a direct extension of traditional views about agency over reproduction in Indigenous nations. This and other such networks reflect Native cultural values manifesting in new ways in contemporary Native spaces. Marriage and divorce practices, birth control and abortion, and the health of the nation by controlling over-reproduction all fell within the purview of Indigenous women in many, if not to some degree in all, Native nations. The threat to the patriarchal system brought by the European settlers could not be clearer, and thus the strategies enacted over centuries that target Native women were more devastating and focused on halting and silencing them. Understanding these practices challenges dominant patriarchal narratives and invites us to reimagine gender equity and reproductive justice through an Indigenous lens. By centering these stories, we honor the resilience of Indigenous women and their ongoing contributions to global conversations about autonomy and communal well-being. Understanding and supporting Indigenous-led reproductive justice movements is essential to decolonizing gendered oppression.

3
What happened? How gendered colonial strategies targeted Indigenous women's bodily sovereignty and harmed the nations

If we get the girls, we get the race.

—Reverend Isaac Baird, Superintendent of the Wisconsin Presbyterian Board of Foreign Missions (an Indian boarding school), founded in 1873[142]

When a Native woman suffers abuse, this abuse is an attack on her identity as a woman and an attack on her identity as Native. The issues of colonial, race, and gender oppression cannot be separated…every Native survivor I ever counseled said to me at one point, "I wish I was no longer Indian".

—Dr Andrea Smith[143]

In mainstream American culture, we do not live by the well-known Cheyenne proverb that reigns throughout Indian Country and is often quoted in Indigenous scholarship. However, the American Founders and many boarding school teachers, government officials, and social leaders understood its meaning very well:

> A people cannot be conquered until the hearts of the women are on the ground. Then it is finished; no matter how brave their warriors or how strong their weapons.

This is why Native American women were historically targeted, and still remain disproportionately impacted, by European colonial ethnic cleansing and sterilization programs, physical attacks, sexual assaults, and wholesale disenfranchisement (often within their own communities): they are the cultural hearts of their people. They are the indispensable women who hold their nations and their people together. They are called the Gantowisas,[144] the Ogimah Ikwe,[145] and the Mindimooyenh[146]—some of the many Indigenous terms used for women who lead.

Attempts to conquer a people require more than military violence and geographic dislocation. Striking at the core of their cultural beliefs is mandatory. Attempts to dismantle social, economic, and governing structures, to render their cosmologies illegitimate and primitive, to remove and brainwash their children, and to promulgate dehumanizing stereotypes in the conquering culture all are necessary to physically diminish and psychologically denigrate a people. The negative results of these practices eventually manifest hopelessness and despair in the colonized people that led to intergenerational trauma, addiction, and inner community violence. These are the tactics of empire used by

European settlers against Native Americans, and they are ongoing today. There is no postcolonial Indigenous state in America; however, there is thriving, robust well-being, cultural continuance, and resiliency amid the struggles in Native nations. This chapter argues that colonial strategies systematically targeted Indigenous women's roles as cultural leaders and biological reproducers to dismantle their nations. By examining historical and contemporary examples, this chapter demonstrates how attacks on women's sovereignty are fundamental to colonial projects and continue to harm Indigenous communities today.

Alarming impacts on Native reproductive health continue. Economic disparities, discriminatory acts, stereotypes, and the remoteness of healthcare facilities all contribute to the disproportionately high rates of reproductive health issues experienced by Native mothers today. A national comprehensive study on American Indian reproductive health was conducted by Frontiers in Public Health, which reported that rates of preterm birth and low birth weight continue to be higher for Native Americans than the Caucasian population.[147] Attorney Lauren van Schilfgaarde (Cochiti Pueblo) of UCLA School of Law wrote in a 2022 Harvard Law blog that the maternal mortality rate of Native women is "1.2 times the rate for non-Hispanic white women" and that Native women "have the least access to emergency contraception and abortion services" in the United States.[148] Along with these statistics, van Schilfgaarde notes that the Hyde Amendment specifically and disproportionately impacts Indigenous women who use Indian Health Services for reproductive care as they "have effectively been living under a total abortion ban for the last forty-five years" when the U.S. Congress passed an amendment in 1976 that prohibited the use of federal funds for abortions. A research study conducted at the University of Chicago by Dr Autumn Asher BlackDeer reports outcomes that 81 percent of Indigenous peoples who identified as holding liberal political views reported they were pro-choice on the issue of abortion.

To successfully dismantle Indigenous nations, Native women had to be cast down from their positions of power. Their voices and status had to be delegitimized and conscripted into the image of the obedient and dutiful woman valued by the European settlers who subjugated women in their own societies. But more importantly, a link between the obedient wife trope had to be made with the concept of a civilized society and divine law, thereby not merely tearing Native women from their national status, but claiming *that women's honorable status itself* was inferior and barbaric. Male supremacy had to be incorporated at all levels of Native society, and in the peoples' consciousness, in order to ensure that Indigenous people themselves would enforce the new world order that placed European ancestry and males at the top of the social hierarchy—and that's exactly what they did. Native women's sexuality, fertility, reproductive agency, and roles in their nations as mothers, both historically and to this day, were critical tools settler policies used to accomplish the task of colonizing Native Americans. How that was achieved is the subject of this chapter.

First, Native motherhood has been historically managed and under attack by the U.S. federal government and its agencies as it set standards of inadequate reproductive healthcare through the Indian Health Service.[149] The second involves the power of motherhood itself. Sociologist Barbara Gurr writes that since "mothers 'both signify and reproduce the symbolic and legal boundaries of the collectivity' by giving birth and socializing children into identity...Native women's motherhood potentially challenges efforts to produce and protect a hegemonically white national family identity, and therefore their productive bodies become a site for the management of Native people by the U.S. government."[150] More specific tools of colonization that attempt to destroy Indigenous nations by targeting Native women's agency include:

- attacks on woman-centered leadership and divinities
- removal of Native women as clan mothers who govern land use
- reeducation of Native children in Indian boarding schools
- forced sterilization of Native women
- extractive industries on Native lands that promote sexual violence against Native teens and women
- adopting out Native children to non-Native parents
- environmental poisoning that impacts fertility
- the passage of tribal laws and doctrines that disenfranchise Native women.

All these together impact Native women's autonomy over their bodies and influence their reproductive controls and, from this, Native nations are diminished and deeply struggle.

Attacks on Indigenous women's leadership and sovereignty

The subjugation of Native traditional cultures that support women's agency could only be accomplished by chipping away at the fundamental rights of Native women's social and spiritual roles in their nations. To secure the inroads that laid a foundation for dislocating the centrality of Indigenous divine creatrixes, like Sky Woman, Changing Woman, Copper Woman, and so forth, Native people had to be ethnically cleansed and partially adopt European religious beliefs. Many nations did so in an attempt to survive colonial encroachments and all-out attacks, but it seldom garnered the results they sought, which included recognition of sovereignty and cultural respect. In many cases, adopting Eurosettler cultural values and practices only aided the disintegration of traditions and created intertribal divisions. Paula Gunn Allen writes that to transform Native American gender-balanced social structures, what she refers to as gynocracies, to a Eurocolonial hierarchical, patriarchal system requires the following:

- Removal and replacement of female creators with male-gendered creators, like the generic "Great Spirit" rather than multiplicitous tribal designations of deities [many of whom are female and Two-Spirited];
- The destruction of tribal governing institutions and philosophies that are replaced with non-Indigenous forms of democracy (powerful officials elected by majority rule, typically men);
- The nations being dislocated from traditional homelands and their systems altered to embrace male-dominated, non-tribal philosophies and rituals; and
- Clan structures are replaced by the nuclear family valuing male headship.[151]

Some key components in this apparatus to alter a balanced social structure included placing a single person (a male) in the role of governing leader, instituting punishments for disobedience, reeducation of the young, and forbidding divorce.[152] In some nations, abortion was outright forbidden and presented as the nation's new prophetic traditions. Much of this reeducation was at first enacted by priests who invaded Indigenous communities with their Christian beliefs that espouse female subjugation as fundamental and paramount in a civilized society. Later the Indian boarding schools played a key role in accomplishing the restructuring of Native societies. In addition, large-scale strategies were undertaken by the European settlers, as in the case of the British influence, to remove women from offices in the Cherokee nation. The British took Cherokee men to England and had them educated in English ways that included male supremacy and Christianity, which divinely endorses it.[153] When the U.S. Congress passed the Indian Removal Act in 1830, these British-educated Cherokee men participated in the disenfranchisement of Cherokee women from governing the nation. The men wrote women out of the Cherokee constitution believing that doing so would protect them from removal. It didn't. The last official Beloved Woman, Nancy Ward, resigned her office in 1817 and sent her cane and her vote to the Cherokee Council and renounced her high office.[154] This led to another step in the removal and displacement of Indigenous women in their own sovereign nations: the Dawes Act, also called the General Allotment Act, of 1887.

The General Allotment Act was passed by the U.S. Congress to break up the ancient Indigenous tribal tradition of nations holding land communally. Individual Native people or families did not own land, but, in most cases, nations understood certain geographic spaces as their territory that the nation used and cared for collectively. Oftentimes, clan mothers decided which clans had use of parcels of land for farming and fishing on a rotating basis across the seasons. Larger geographic spaces outside the immediate territories of most Native nations were shared, open lands that Indigenous peoples traveled through, hunted, and harvested foods and medicinal plants. In this way, Indigenous nations used land that reflected their way of understanding themselves as a cohesive people with a shared cultural identity and, thus, responsibility to the community through respectful land use. Knowing this full well, the Americans strategized to destroy that cohesive, cultural identity reflected in collective land use/ownership by passing the Dawes Act. President Teddy Roosevelt said in 1901 that America should see "the Indian as an individual and not as a member of a tribe" and lauded the General Allotment Act as "a mighty pulverizing engine to break up the tribal mass".[155] The act demanded that not only individual Native Americans should own land, but that primarily males should be heads-of-households, thus displacing Indigenous women. Also, the act opened the floodgates to non-Native ownership of Native lands, and mass dispossession of tribal spaces led to land grabbing by settlers. This act not only undermined communal land use but displaced Indigenous women from their traditional roles as land stewards and decision-makers, disrupting the very foundation of Gender Complementary governance.

Indian boarding schools and cultural disruption

As I discussed in Chapter 2, Indigenous girls in many nations participated in complex menarche rituals that prepared them for their roles in the community as adult women. These rituals carried deep psychological messages to the girls about their value as females and the nation-specific types of responsibilities toward their people because of that femaleness. The girls' coming-of-age ceremonies signified profound meaning to the entire nation regardless of others' gender identity: human women reflect the duty and spiritual power represented in the divine creatrix of their people and of the larger cosmology as they understand it. Respect, honor, purpose, importance, and responsibility are all terms that can describe the complex meanings inherent in these ceremonies—and those meanings were transmitted to everyone in the nation about females. Therefore, the rituals at once promulgated gendered meanings about being female while also preparing the girls to serve their people and continue their cultures, their ancestor's teachings, and their very existence as a people.

Policymakers at the U.S. Bureau of Indian Affairs in the late 1800s knew this cultural fact about Native girls, as did the Protestant ministers and Catholic priests and nuns who ran the Indian boarding schools. The gender disparity was recognized by leaders in the boarding schools, noting that they "had a difficult time securing students, especially girls" as Native people "feared to give up their girls…not trusting the white people".[156] Because of this cultural knowledge about the importance of girls in Native cultures, Native girls were specifically targeted by these settler institutions to be brought into the boarding schools and ethnically cleansed through indoctrination to Victorian values for females: submission to males at every conceivable level (especially in a nuclear family where he is head of household), Christianization, domesticity, sexual shaming, heteronormativity, unfettered childbearing, and political and economic silence. Textbooks at the schools taught those values. At the Hampton Institute in Virginia, a historic photograph shows Native girls dressed as Victorian ladies in long dresses and making "charcoal portraits of a boy dressed [in] his Plains warrior best".[157] This indoctrination could not be in greater contrast to the teachings and communal responsibilities Indigenous girls are taught in most coming-of-age ceremonies that understand that girls reflect the image of their divine creator, their bodily functions are sacred and powerful, and they are expected to step into roles deeply supporting their people in ways that demonstrate strength and their intellect. The boarding schools' mission was not only to utterly erase those concepts in Native girls that were deemed savagery but to ensure they never learned them. Anthropologist Carol Devens writes, "A [Native] girl's exposure to Anglo-American religious, economic, and gender values [in boarding schools] often had a permanent effect on her, whether or not she accepted them" and that time spent at these schools interrupted key relationship building and instruction of girls by their female relatives that placed them as women within their "own cultural traditions".[158] Dakota ethnographer Ella Deloria's 1988 writings are cited as well, as they document the critical role older women/grandmothers played in a young Native girl's cultural upbringing that was essential for her to flourish in her nation as a woman.[159]

Devens relies heavily on the primary source evidence from Dakota author and activist Zitkala-sa's important autobiographical work titled *American Indian Stories* about her time at the Indian boarding school in the 1880s. In a contemporary memoir,

Lakota author Mary Crow Dog writes of her experience at St Francis Boarding School in South Dakota in the 1960s with similar dismay. Crow Dog writes that "[t]he girls' wing…was run like a penal institution" with 5 am Christian prayers on their knees and being "herded into church" and "marching by the clock".[160] The beatings and punishments of girls were sexualized, as she notes that teenaged girls who were old enough to menstruate and have babies had their skirts lifted up and underpants pulled down by nuns before they beat them.[161] For running away, girls were stripped naked, whipped with buggy whips, and placed in cells in the school's attic during Crow Dog's grandmother's time at St Francis. Nuns used sexualized and shaming language in the dormitories for the girls huddling in bed together saying "I smell evil in this room. You girls are evil incarnate. You are sinning… You can act that way in the devil's frying pan". They then made the girls kneel and pray all night. Crow Dog writes incredulously that "[w]e had not the slightest idea what it was all about. At home we slept two and three in a bed for animal warmth and a feeling of security".[162]

Boarding school attendance and colonial indoctrination severed the emotional, psychological, and cultural bonds between Indigenous mothers and daughters—and between girls and their older female relatives—creating a deep cultural chasm within Indigenous nations. By breaking the bonds between Indigenous girls and their matrilineal teachings, boarding schools disrupted the cultural practices that sustained nations, leaving a legacy of loss and disconnection that many communities are still working to heal. Being prevented from experiencing traditional menarche rituals and learning social norms from female relatives was devastating to Native girls and their many cultures their existence promulgated. Though culturally distinct in their practices, most Indigenous nations are founded on communal interdependence; hence, having half of the nation not functioning within their cultural purview would be devastating overall and would surely impact non-female people as well. Of course, boys were indoctrinated too, which greatly impacted the nations. Further, because of the centrality of females in many Native nations, the whole community's ability to express itself fully as a people would be deeply harmed; this legacy would ensure debilitation for generations to come. Reconceptualizing what it means to be a Native girl and a woman, and the subsequent responsibilities to one's Native nation as such, was a colonial strategy that used gender specifically tied to the reproductive functions of females to attempt to destroy their cultures. Preventing Native girls from participating in their menarche rituals, reshaping how they understand themselves as culturally valuable women, turning female physical contact into sexualized shame, and expecting Victorian submission to men and domesticity impacted Native nations in devastating ways that continue until today. Though the term "bodily sovereignty" is unlikely to be linguistically present among Indigenous nations historically, the concept itself is embedded in girls' menstrual rituals. In Indian boarding school curricula, and in the version of western culture the European settlers brought with them in general, the concept of female bodily autonomy barely existed beyond clear restrictions (like heterosexual sex is allowed for women, but only within marriage, for example).

The impact of the Indian boarding schools on Two-Spirited people cannot be overstated as it continues to this day in the bias against LGBTQ people by those Native children, now elders, who were indoctrinated at the schools. Homophobia and shaming of LGBTQ Native people are common in Indian Country, as much as there is a movement for Two-Spirit inclusion and celebration. Reclaiming lesbian and gay sexuality, identities, and histories is part of the recovery of overall Indigenous identity and cultural continuance. Without the acknowledgment of Two-Spirit experiences, no Native history can be complete, and no sovereignty can be fully realized and expressed. Adding to this, at boarding schools, sexual violations and shaming in general, and lesbian and gay sexual persecution specifically, continue to keep Two-Spirits closeted and silenced. This is why the effects of colonization continue today, and we are not in a postcolonial state, by any means.

Forced sterilizations and reproductive coercion

Along with the displacement of Indigenous women's roles in their nations and reeducation at Indian boarding schools, direct attacks on their reproductive agency were rampant in the 1970s. Many Indigenous communities in the United States have their primary access to healthcare facilities and practitioners through the Indian Health Service (IHS) hospitals, which have been funded through the division of the Health, Education, and Welfare department since 1955. These facilities are typically located in Indigenous communities that are in geographically remote areas, which increases patients' vulnerability and prevents access to better services. Between 1970 and 1976, as various studies demonstrated, 25–50 percent of Native American women and teens using these facilities were sterilized without their consent by doctors at the IHS.[163] For example, two teenage girls went to an IHS in Montana for appendectomies and also received tubal ligations without their, or their parents', knowledge or consent.[164] Across Indian Country, this became a common occurrence and Native people filed allegations against the IHS for failure to provide women with information about sterilization; use of coercion to get signatures on consent forms; improper consent forms; and lack of a waiting period between signing a consent form and a surgical procedure.[165] Fears that their children would be taken away from them[166] and/or that benefits would be discontinued were common reasons Indigenous women signed consent forms—when forms were even provided. The fact that these forms were written in English and not their Indigenous language was another issue. Another tactic doctors used to coerce women into sterilization was leading them to believe that the form they were signing during childbirth was for pain medication; alternately, these women were pressured to sign the forms *after* the procedure was already completed.[167] Between 1973 and 1976, the IHS performed 3,406 sterilizations; however, sterilizations at other IHS facilities were not counted.

The primary reason the Euro-American male physicians engaged in these immoral acts was they were motivated by economic and social beliefs about America's welfare burden created by low-income, minority families.[168] More specifically, they believed that Native American women were not intelligent enough to use birth control; that they were creating social unrest in the nation through the American Indian Movement; and the doctors wanted to gain gynecological experience at the government's (and the Native women's) expense.[169]

The cost to Native women for these forced sterilizations was devastating—both personally and to their communities. Dissolution of marriages, friendships, and families over sterilizations were common, along with psychological issues, drug use, and shame.[170] While forced sterilization programs disproportionately targeted young women seen as potential reproducers of Indigenous nations, older women were often targeted for their roles as cultural transmitters and healers. The multigenerational impact of these policies underscores the adaptability of patriarchal violence to various social contexts. As a community, the tribal impact was significant as well, as census numbers determine representation not only at the state and national levels for elected officials but also within the tribal councils.[171] But, perhaps, more importantly, the value of children to Native people cannot be overstated in terms of tribal survival and the mothers' place in the nation. In 2024, *The Lancet* reported that the life expectancy of Native Americans is 64 years, which is 20 years fewer than Asian Americans who hold the highest longevity rates in the United States.[172]

In addition to these coercive sterilization practices, "sterilization among Native women continues to be high…in 2004, 33.9 percent of Native women were using tubal ligation as a form of contraception", which is outrageously higher than the statistic for any other U.S. demographic.[173] Many Native women opt for tubal ligation, which is permanent, because this is the only reliable means of birth control available to them. The reasons for this include having insufficient funds to purchase other forms of birth control, not having regular access to a car to drive to an IHS facility to get the birth control, other forms of birth control being unavailable at the IHS, and experiencing pressure from partners that disrupt women's agency.

Environmental violence and extractive industries

Extractive industries are involved in the removal of timber, gas, and oil deposits on or near lands governed by Native American tribes. Extractive industries create what are called "man camps" as thousands of male workers come to geographically remote areas to work in the industries. In addition to the workers, often ex-military personnel are given access to state and federal jobs at these sites to police them, which creates highly aggressive interactions between them, Native people, and Native tribal police. The employees of these industries work long days, are isolated in temporary trailer parks, and are socially disconnected from friends, families, and communities for months, even years. These camps then become centers for drugs, sex trafficking, and violence. Tragically, Native American women and teens are often primary targets at these sites as they are adjacent to, on, or near their communities. The 2017 film *Wind River* depicted such a tragedy. The organization Missing and Murdered Indigenous Women and Girls (MMIWG) addresses the widespread problem of Native American and First Nations of Canada females being targeted for violence and sexual assault by non-Indigenous perpetrators. The Violence Against Women Act of 1994 allows tribal councils to prosecute non-Native offenders on tribal lands. However, it is still a complex legal problem involving questions of jurisdiction, the roles of tribal and non-tribal law officers, and the persistent dehumanization of Indigenous women—rooted in colonial tropes that portray them as inherently violable. Native American women have higher rates of sexual violence than any other demographic, and the violence is more severe. In addition, while overall perpetrators of sexual violence tend to be of the same race and ethnicity as their victims, this is not the case for Native females. Nearly 88 percent of violence against Native American women are committed by non-Natives.[174] The violence Indigenous women face near man camps exemplifies how colonial systems continue to exploit both their bodies and their lands, perpetuating cycles of harm.

Andrea Smith's critical book on Native women and sexual violence, titled *Conquest*, notes that "[b]ecause Indian bodies are 'dirty,' they are considered sexually violable and 'rapable', and the rape of bodies that are considered inherently impure or dirty simply does not count".[175] In the narrative of America that is promulgated about Indigenous people and colonial history, Indians are understood as non-Christian savages who need to be expunged from the country to protect American society, and especially Euro-American people. In the language I have already cited from Indian boarding school teachers, the concept that Native people, especially girls and women, are dirty is widespread. Smith pointedly asserts that the "U.S. colonizers view the subjugation of women of the Native nations as critical to the success of the economic, cultural, and political colonization" of the country and that "Native women are bearers of a counter-imperial order and pose a supreme threat to the dominant culture."[176] Hence, villainizing them through denigrating images in popular culture, through distorted historical narratives, and through invented, but authoritative, anthropological discourse, powerfully constructs a very real experience justifying settler-on-Native acts of violence that perpetrators deem entirely justifiable. Therefore, through sexual attacks on Indigenous women, the heart of the nations are made vulnerable, and this further weakens Indigenous sovereignty. Smith notes that "Native women reproduce the next generation of Native people", and this fact is a threat to governmental agencies and corporations that eye Native lands for extractive resources where much of the U.S. reserves of oil and gas are found.[177] In this way, Indigenous women, their pregnancies, and their children are a threat to privileged elites.

Moreover, the bodies and fertility of Indigenous women are severely impacted by environmental toxins present on their lands through military testing and storage of weapons, extractive industries for oil and gas, and mining for coal and uranium. The following are a few examples of a widespread problem across a century of time in North American Indigenous nations. To begin, the Western Shoshone Nation has recorded over 600 nuclear weapon explosions on their lands by the U.S. government since the 1960s. The Indigenous lands of Hawaiian Islanders are a storage site for tens of thousands of nuclear weapons.[178] In the Marshall Islands in the Pacific, military weapons more powerful than the atomic bombs dropped on Hiroshima and Nagasaki in World War II were tested; this led to devastating birth defects among the Indigenous population.[179] Native women there gave birth to "jellyfish babies" (babies with no bones) and one in three births in the Marshall Islands between 1954 and 1958 resulted in fetal death.[180] In other Indigenous lands, rates of cancer incidence, miscarriages, and birth defects are astronomical in comparison to national averages.[181] Mohawk midwife Katsi Cook in upstate New York has reported that, for decades, environmental poisons dumped into their waters are passed to Mohawk children through breastmilk.[182] Last, the Indigenous advocacy group Women of All Red Nations has, for half a century, warned of the devastating effects of radiation on Indigenous women's bodies, including spontaneous abortion and cancer mortality; they have urged Indigenous women to "Defend Your Unborn" in an *Akwesasne Notes* article back in 1980.[183] What these statistics demonstrate is the multiplicitous fight Native people wage to protect Indigenous women's fertility and the lives of their children, and another form of colonial attacks on Indigenous women, their reproductive powers, and thus tribal sovereignty.

Contemporary challenges to sovereignty and reproductive justice

Nations that are structured around clans and kinship networks look radically different when it comes to parenting children than a nuclear family structure does. Being surrounded daily by blood relatives and spiritually bonded people ensures Native children have the nurturance and guidance of many adults to meet their complex developmental and spiritual needs. "Indian children are never alone. They are always surrounded by grandparents, uncles, cousins, relatives of all kinds, who fondle the kids, sing to them, tell them stories. If the parents go someplace, the kids go along", writes Lakota Medicine Man John (Fire) Lame Deer

(1903–1976).[184] A generation later, Mary Crow Dog writes nearly verbatim that in traditional Sioux families

> the child is never left alone. It is always surrounded by relatives, carried around, enveloped in warmth. It is treated with respect…seldom screamed at, and never beaten. And then suddenly a bus or car arrives, full of strangers, usually white strangers…taking it screaming to the boarding school…kidnapping.[185]

The late Mohegan Medicine Woman Gladys Tantaquidgeon wrote of her time working for the Bureau of Indian Affairs in South Dakota in the 1930s about Native children being removed to boarding school as an "effective way of breaking the tribe's spirit".[186] Tantaquidgeon noted how Native families in the communities she served hid their children from government workers. During one visit to a Native family, she observed thus: "I saw the hand of one small child poking out from under the bed, and another was in a corner somewhere. So I told [the parents] I was not out to punish them or tell other school officials."[187] However, these practices were not isolated to the Plains Indian nations, but were widespread in the United States. For example, in Connecticut, where some of the traditional homelands of the Mohegan nation are located, Indigenous children "were expected to learn English and forget all about their Indian cultural background [in school]". Consequently, Mohegan elders would not speak their language in front of the children out of fear the kids would be punished.[188]

Fear of child abduction and ethnic cleansing in Indian boarding schools was a pervasive presence in Native communities for centuries, but the problem escalated only in the 1900s and persists in various forms today. This is a form of colonial attack that targets Indigenous women's roles in their nations as mothers of the nations with the power to protect their children and tribes. When non-Indigenous social workers enter Native communities, inquire about a Native child's biological parents, and ascertain that they are not living in the home, a case is typically opened and the child removed. This is the imposition of western cultural values that understand legal guardians and biological parents as the sole caretakers of children. This may be so in mainstream American culture, but those concepts and values do not apply in Indigenous communities.

Mass displacement of Native American children has been a threat since colonial times and continued into the 1970s unabated as children were taken from Indigenous families and clans and placed into adoption agencies and foster care. A 1970s study shows that "25–35% of all Native children were being removed" from their families and "85% were placed outside their families and communities".[189] In the 1930s, there was a colonial practice called "kid catching" of Native children by "stockmen, police, farmers, and mounted men who came on [the Navajo] reservation to literally round up school-age children to attend faraway government boarding schools".[190] Food was also used by religious and government agencies as a lure to bring in hungry children to be coerced and kidnapped to attend boarding schools. This was a widespread problem across the United States and Canada. The Cree First Nations artist Kent Monkman powerfully depicts this North American practice in his 2017 painting titled "The Scream".

A significant contributor to the horror of Indigenous child abduction was the Mormon Church. They had a placement program specifically for Indigenous children who were seen by them as cursed by God, dark and loathsome sinners, and Lamenites (the lost tribe of Israel) needing to be saved.[191] Approximately 2,000 Native children were taken *annually* from their homes by the Mormons.[192] Considering that in a 1971 Indian boarding school census it was determined that approximately 35,000 Native children at that time lived away from their families and communities, action was taken by Indigenous advocates and policymakers to stem the catastrophe wrought by state social workers and government officials.[193] Monetary motivation to remove vulnerable Native children whose parents have little social power must be factored into this centuries-long problem. The Federal Title IV-E law provides up to 80 percent, or more in some cases, in reimbursement to state programs and tribes to cover the costs of foster care, administration of state programs, and training of employees.[194] So the more children enter foster care, the more money will be brought into the state system via federal dollars.

The outcome of years of Indigenous lobbying, advocacy, and congressional hearings resulted in the passing of the Indian Child Welfare Act (ICWA) of 1978. The purpose of this federal law, signed by President Jimmy Carter, was to ensure the preservation of Indigenous cultures and races and to protect Native children from adoption or fostering out by non-Native parents.[195] Under this law, Native children must be placed with extended family to maintain their cultures, and the tribes must have a voice in the fostering, custody, and adoption processes.[196] However, there remains one concerning caveat: due to powerful political influencers, the Mormon Church was excluded from the federal law and was allowed to continue adopting Native children through its placement program![197]

Problems challenging the authority of the ICWA continue today, unfortunately, as in Haaland v. Brackeen from 2023, which was a U.S. Supreme Court case brought by the states of Texas, Louisiana, and Indiana, and individual plaintiffs, that sought to declare the ICWA unconstitutional.[198] The Native American Rights Fund that was involved in the case points out the motivations behind challenging the ICWA: "In the past several years, anti-tribal interests have launched a series of legal challenges against ICWA, with the goal of broadly undermining tribal sovereignty."[199]

In another example of contemporary attacks that ignore and attempt to bypass the ICWA to remove Indigenous children from their families, the American Civil Liberties Union (ACLU) represented the Oglala Sioux and Rosebud Sioux nations in 2013 on behalf of Native families in Pennington County South Dakota. The complaint alleged that

> [s]tate employees were removing children from their homes and then holding hearings in state court within 48 hours, in which parents were not assigned counsel to represent them, were not given a copy of the petition accusing them of wrongdoing, and no state employee was called to testify. Moreover, the parents were not permitted to testify, call witnesses, or cross-examine any state employee. The hearings typically lasted fewer than five minutes—some were done in 60 seconds—and the state won 100 percent of the time. Native children would remain in foster care for two months or longer before their parents were given an opportunity to challenge the removal at a subsequent hearing.[200]

The ACLU's case prevailed in protecting Indigenous children in this county, but ongoing attempts to chip away at Indigenous sovereignty in decision-making about child welfare continue. When concerns about a child's welfare arise—as they do in all communities across the United States—the ICWA mandates that Indigenous extended families and tribal councils make key decisions about Native children, rather than non-Indigenous state workers. But when these officials look through the lens of western culture, they see neglect when a Native child is surrounded by its blood- and spiritually bonded relatives and not by its biological parents. Though some state social workers and government officials are somewhat benignly engaging in ethnocentric assessments with good intentions (in their eyes) about Indigenous children, the end result is the same as those who strategically remove Native kids to "save" them from being Indian and engage in western-cultural exceptionalism that includes imposing Christianity. And that end result is a means to eliminate Indigenous cultural knowledges and the sense Native people have of being a people. By ensuring that Indigenous children remain within their communities, ICWA safeguards not only individual children, but more importantly, it also protects the intergenerational transmission of cultural knowledge and thus the survival of tribal nations.

Native women's leadership and barriers from within Native nations

Undermining Indigenous women's traditional roles in their nations historically came not only from outside colonial sources, but eventually made inroads into Native systems and contaminated long-standing norms, beliefs, and practices involving women at all levels of their existence. Leadership is a culture-based concept. It is valued and practiced differently in cultures that centralize individual gains (capitalist, western culture) rather than interdependent, communal ethics (Indigenous). Spirituality, the values of generosity and honoring all living beings, and serving one's community with humility and by example (not authority) are but a few components of Indigenous leadership styles.[201] Importantly, the singularity of one leader ruling the entire nation was, and often remains, anathema to Indigenous people who function under cultural concepts centralizing the community, not individual power.

Corporate feminism is an academic concept that looks at ways females make gains in the workplace; it centralizes individual advancement and financial gain for women as a means to equity and greater social power. However, there is no corollary among traditional Indigenous women's leadership goals and styles. Instead, leadership for Native women is similar to roles of women as caregivers and nurturers,[202]—concepts that contemporary feminism criticizes as narrow, even subjugated, gender roles for women. Indeed, the end of gender roles altogether, and, to some, the end to gender identity itself, is expressly called for by some contemporary feminists. These individuals and movements seem to have no knowledge of Indigenous complementary social structures that sustained communal equity for millennia and demonstrate, unequivocally, that neither gender roles nor gender itself are the problems with gender bias in the world today.

Of the nearly 600 federally recognized tribes in the United States, about 20 percent, or 120, are led by Native women,[203] but tribal chauvinism and gender bias play a role in Native women's leadership today.[204] The late Cherokee Chief Wilma Mankiller recounts that when she was running for office, the sentiment of many in her nation was that they would be a laughingstock of the tribes if they elected a female chief.[205] She recounts the hate mail, death threats, and open hostility she received from male and female tribal members, though "the most vicious [were] from men" who were belligerent about being supervised by a woman.[206] Horizontal violence originating from both Native women and men colleagues was also reported by women leaders in one study, who noted that college trustees, tribal council leaders, and an attorney deliberately sabotaged and attacked these Native women leaders to prevent them from being promoted or from fulfilling their duties as high-ranking leaders, like a college presidency. One Native woman from the study reported that she was accused of being "too bossy and not acting like an Indian".[207] What this information demonstrates is the devastating impact on Indigenous women caused by their own nations that have been corrupted by colonial misogyny, and the outcomes of empire to dysregulate an entire people around gender.

Contemporary Native women often must fight their own people for respect, inclusion, and leadership roles, as well as for the protection of reproductive health and their children. The former Lakota Chief Cecelia Fire Thunder was called an "extreme feminazi"[208] by one of her constituents for lobbying for a wellness center to provide reproductive healthcare, including abortion, on the Pine Ridge Reservation in South Dakota. Access to abortion there was severely limited at the time, especially for Native teens and women, and is now illegal altogether. In some nations, reproductive controls were codified into law. Barbara Mann writes that "the freedom with which Iroquoian women resorted to abortion was singled out for condemnation [by the Seneca prophet Handsome Lake]…in one of its main woman-crushing innovations" that was preached by him in 1840.[209] Mann continues by noting that "the Clan Mothers were not willing to put up with such 'white' talk as a male ban on a female function" and that Handsome Lake's position was "politically motivated, evidence of its unpopularity with the Clan Mothers".[210] Over centuries, as the clan mothers became increasingly disempowered due to the poisoning of colonial gender bias against them, prohibitions against abortion took hold in the nation but were not at all followed "slavishly" by Iroquoian women and abortifacients were still concocted and used.[211] The Code of Handsome Lake is often cited as proof positive that outlawing abortion is traditional in the Iroquoian nation, but that is clearly disputed and not in keeping with cultural norms set forth in their traditional stories and constitutional law.

Summary

The consequences of direct colonial strategies (like in Indian boarding schools) and indirect policies (like bomb testing and nuclear storage sites on Native lands) targeting Indigenous women and girls have powerfully impacted fertility rates, reproductive efficacy, and the health of Indigenous children in complex and lasting ways. The intergenerational impacts of nonconsensual, coerced sterilization of Native teens and women, and the removal, adopting-out, and reeducation of Native children, to name but a few issues addressed in this chapter, all have immeasurable and complex impacts on Indigenous nations today. Altogether, they create a hostile social, political, economic, spiritual, and cultural environment for Native American peoples that they must constantly deconstruct and fight outside and inside their nations and, at times, themselves. For literally centuries, the wombs of Native women have been a target of colonial policies that have attempted to topple women from their seats of influence in their nations in order to undo the traditional webs of cultural practices that sustain their people. Federal laws have been passed (like ICWA) and U.S. Supreme Court cases have been won by Native organizations to protect their people, but the fight is never over. Indigenous lands and resources remain coveted by the U.S. government and by powerful corporations and individuals. An important way to acquire these lands is by weakening the nations' sovereignty, eliminating Native peoples themselves, and attacking Native identity. Native mothers are on the frontlines of those assaults and also are the fighters protecting their people and their nations. As Mary Crow Dog laments in her autobiography, "I am a woman of the Red Nation...That is not easy."[212] But Indigenous women's leadership today counters the legacy of colonial violence. For example, movements like Missing and Murdered Indigenous Women and Girls (MMIWG) and reproductive justice organizations like the Native Youth Sexual Health Network continually upend colonial attempts to halt Native progress. Understanding the historical and ongoing assaults on Indigenous women's sovereignty demands not only acknowledgment but action. By centering Indigenous women's voices and leadership in conversations about reproductive justice, environmental protection, and sovereignty, we can work toward repairing the harms of colonial violence and ensuring a future where Indigenous nations thrive. Awareness is the first step, which is a goal of this book. Acting by supporting legislation and policy to protect Native people is the next one.

4
Stealing back the thunder: Indigenous communities decolonizing reproduction and motherhood

> We [the Ojibwe people] respected women who assumed demanding economic and cultural roles, and we deferred to a power and authority that seemed to grow even more concentrated with age and maturity.[213]
>
> —Dr Brenda Child (Red Lake Ojibwe)

> Keep your white hands off my brown body![214]
>
> —Former Lakota Chief Cecelia Fire Thunder

> Indian women and men are not very worried about unmarried mothers and illegitimate children and

receptivity to family-planning services. They point with pride to the growing and high birthrate among Native American populations.[215]

—Dr Rayna Green

To regain lost ground in the movement to protect Indigenous women's reproduction and the complex social, spiritual, and political meanings of "mothering" among the nations, Native women are strengthening and asserting their traditional gendered practices that were in place before European colonization of the Americas. Since colonization, some of those practices had been hidden for protection and preservation and practiced covertly, some had been openly attacked by colonial policies and abolished, while others had been corrupted by Indian boarding school indoctrination and suppressed for the nations' survival. As Paula Gunn Allen declared decades ago: when the evil comes, the beauty will be taken away and hidden until it is safe for it to be openly expressed once again. Indigenous women have been doing the work of protecting their nations and striving to recover their traditions for centuries.

For Indigenous communities, colonization continues, uninterrupted, yoked consequentially and literally to the policies and histories of the colonizers from centuries ago. This remains a sharp truth on the issue of biological reproduction and mothering among Native women and people who birth.

Organizations with grassroots programs supporting sexual and reproductive health for Native Americans abound in Indian Country today to measure and combat the effects of those policies, while simultaneously creating positive paths toward healing. This final chapter will discuss Indigenous cultural ways of conceptualizing motherhood and feminism and how those practices impact reproductive health. I will also include some representative Indigenous programs and organizations that protect reproductive health. Cumulatively, these actions across the United States and Canada are strengthening women's traditional roles in their nations as a way forward to protect Indigenous sovereignty for Native women, children, men, and Two-Spirited people. The primary focus of all Indigenous people's endeavors is nurturing the rising generations of Indigenous youth for a vital decolonized future.

Indigenous feminisms

Indigenous feminism challenges patriarchal hierarchies by emphasizing relationality, ecological interconnectedness, and communal responsibilities. Unlike western feminist frameworks centered on individual rights, Indigenous feminism foregrounds the sovereignty of families, clans, and nations as essential to achieving gender equity. To many Native American people, Indigenous feminism is about equity among all people and the elimination of oppression and marginalization based on gender. The concept goes beyond advocacy for only women and girls—though most Native women are quick to point out that misogyny is now rampant in their communities as an effect of European colonization and is something they must grapple with. Indigenous feminism is about the recovery of Native women's traditional roles in their nations. This means that Indigenous feminisms must be understood within the cultural context of the individual nations. For example, there are offices for women specific to certain nations, like Clan Mother, Jigonsaseh, Beloved Woman, and the like, and thus roles for women must be recovered within those traditional contexts, not just broadly as "women's rights". Also, Indigenous feminisms focus on issues relevant to many Indigenous nations, and they are often very different from feminist focuses in mainstream American culture. Protection of ancestral lands and holy places as well as creatures (like salmon, buffalo, and cedar trees who are revered relatives to certain nations) come under the protective advocacy of Indigenous feminisms. Fundamentally, Indigenous feminisms is about traditional responsibility to the collective through the cultural values of individual Native nations, while simultaneously recognizing the similar ways colonization impacts the nations. Indigenous feminisms also addresses the negative impact of colonial tropes and stereotypes about Native men and how they affect Native women, children, and communities. For example, the common trope about Native men as violent savages is still promulgated through sports mascots and, historically, was widespread in American films. Not having humanistic representation of Native men in popular culture is psychologically damaging to them just as the Indian princess trope is to Native women and girls. For Two-Spirited people, their invisibility in American culture in terms of representation is equally damaging.

Mainstream American feminism and Indigenous feminisms

The rise in America of the concept of female agency and equity originates with Indigenous nations and was modeled for Euro-American women in what is called the First Wave of feminism in the mid-1800s. Sally Roesch Wagner has been writing extensively over the past 50 years about the early suffragists (Mathilda Joslyn Gage, Elizabeth Cady Stanton, and so forth), and their relationships with Indigenous women of the Iroquois nation in upstate New York. Unfortunately, this history is still not widely taught in academia, not even in Women and Gender Studies programs. Diné/Navajo scholar Laura Tohe addresses the concept of feminism directly and invokes with linguistic evidence that "there is no word for feminism in my language".[216] This is because, in most Indigenous nations, women did not need to fight for political power or socioeconomic equity—until the Europeans brought their anti-female laws and practices with them and colonized the Americas. Tohe observes thus:

> My female relatives lived their lives within the Diné matrilineal culture that valued, honored, and respected them. These women passed on to their daughters not only their strength, but the expectation to assume responsibility for the family, and therefore were expected to act as leaders for the family and the tribe. Despite five hundred years of Western patriarchal intrusion, this practice continues.[217]

Tohe recognizes that the matriarchal structure of her people was put in place by the "principal mythological deity in the Diné culture" who is Changing Woman or White Shell Woman.[218] But the type of influence, responsibility, and spiritual representation in Indigenous nations is not what eventually got translated to mainstream American concepts of feminism. That brand of feminism tends to be more individualistic and is motivated by individual gains for American women (like in corporate feminism discussed previously) and is not communal based. In addition, there is deep criticism of gender roles in mainstream American feminism and even contempt for any gender identification at all, as if that is the problem causing anti-female and toxic masculine concepts in western cultural practices historically. In Indigenous nations, gender roles are not a problem as they do not oppress, narrowly define, or restrict personal expression based on gender. Instead, gender is a reflection of much larger principles based on the natural world and cosmos that many Indigenous nations structure their governing systems around to maintain order in their societies. There is no equivalent in American feminism, although, certainly, social equity for all is the bedrock of that feminism.

First Nations scholar Sarah Nickel asserts that Indigenous feminisms differ from white second-wave feminism because it often centralized motherhood. Homemaking is a position of power and empowerment rather than oppressive, as it was (and still is) often posited in Euro-American feminism.[219] This is for legitimate reasons, of course. In addition, Nickel points out that Native women resisted male-dominated leaders' mandates that claimed Native women's rights undermine overall Indigenous rights and therefore Native women who challenge male authority are seen as traitors.[220] This application of Indigenous feminism acknowledges the complexities of Native women who at once are protecting their nations from colonialism while also acknowledging the male violence against them in their own nations.

Last, Indigenous feminism is ultimately about Native sovereignty and the legal rights that the nations have to engage their traditions and protect their lands. As colonial attacks on gender were foundational to dismantling the nations, the antidote to reinstating traditions and shoring up sovereignty lies in returning Indigenous women to their critical roles in their nations—roles they have always held, though expressed in diverse ways across nations. Some Native activists refute feminism as being relevant for Indigenous people, while still others observe that an Indigenous-brand of feminism is the tool needed to meet the critical goal of protecting Native nations and lands. Notably, Andrea Smith points out that gaining sovereignty alone is not going to undo rampant gender violence and misogyny in Indigenous nations.[221] Thus, those issues must be addressed together as advocates of all identities, not solely Indigenous, work toward a sustainable future for the nations.[222]

Indigenous feminism has been defined by some Native women as "a multisphered concept with the family as the center, surrounded by clan identification, then tribe and tribal relationships, which can mean relationships with state and federal governments", while still others (with the addition of Gloria Steinem's words) point out that "[f]eminism is also history and even memory".[223] Andrea Smith importantly expands on the concept of memory and specifically asserts that Native feminism must hold a discussion that "incorporates remembering…pre-colonial egalitarian gender systems", and this is not simply to raise the status of Native women, but of their nations to benefit everyone.[224] Finally, as many Indigenous activists, writers, and artists note, fundamentally Indigenous feminism is about promoting tribal sovereignty, protecting Mother Earth, and empowering Native women to accomplish those endeavors. Reproductive protection is one of those goals.

Indigenous motherhood as anti-colonial political power

Indigenous women have strategically maintained their traditional political roles as mothers of the nations despite external colonial pressure and internal censorship by their own people. Over centuries, they created groups to hide their traditional roles in plain sight or reimagine the expression of their traditions in safe ways so their people could flourish. From the Mohegan nation's Church Ladies Sewing Society on the American east coast to First Nations of British Columbia's Indian Homemakers' Club on the other side of Turtle Island, Native women have always found ways to keep doing what needed to be done.

On the East Coast, to continue the work of running the nation without appearing as an outright threat to the state, women leaders in the Mohegan nation began the Church Ladies Sewing Society in Connecticut. It was first led by Emma Tyler Fielding Baker (1828–1916) and functioned similarly to a traditional women's council. Mohegan historian Melissa Fawcett writes that "the tribe's ancient matriarchy had chosen this group as their new venue".[225] The women "considered potential new chiefs, discussed land claims, and evaluated promising children", along with crafting tribal society and politics.[226] An important function of this group was planning for the all-important annual Wigwam festival, especially because "non-Indian ways had spread among the people", and the Wigwam was falling out of practice and replaced by Christian practices.[227] The society revived the festival and built a brush arbor at the church on Mohegan land, as they knew the Wigwam "could only survive in coexistence with the church".²²⁸ Fawcett points out that the Elders "didn't think of [the festival] in terms of 'Mohegan Indian cultural survival'...[t]hat was just part of everyday life".²²⁹ In this way, the traditional roles of women as mothers of the nation continued, but this should not be understood simply as "women's power" as an end unto itself. Rather, Mohegan women, and almost all Indigenous women, assert their traditional roles for the protection of their children, ancestral knowledge, and the nations, and that includes protecting Native men.

The Indigenous Women's Network, Women of All Red Nations, and, currently, the National Indigenous Women's Resource Center (NIWRC) all play a contemporary role in furthering traditional roles for Indigenous women as they advocate for the land and their nations. Indigenous Women's Network and Women of All Red Nations (WARN) are two long-standing Native women-led organizations that promote Indigenous women's sovereignty to empower cultural traditions and their nations. WARN was founded by Native women in 1974 and, although they have many goals in their mission statement and policies, protecting Indigenous women's reproductive rights is part of their platform. One of WARN's many significant accomplishments was to raise awareness about attacks on Native women's health in the 1970s and 1980s. Today, they remain active in advocating for the protection of Native land rights, like protesting the Keystone oil pipeline running through sacred Dakota lands. The NIWRC is holding a 2025 conference titled "Women Are Sacred", which will offer "state-of-the-art training and networking opportunities designed to increase the capacity of Tribal Nations, Tribal domestic violence, and community-based programs to address violence in Tribal communities".[230] Advocacy for the nations began centuries ago and has continued, uninterrupted, across generations and time.

Another example of the politically strategic roles of Indigenous mothers is from the 1950s in the British Columbia Indian Homemakers' Club. This group of mothers used gatherings as political movements to share wisdom and encourage women's leadership. They eventually began addressing poor conditions in their communities created by the Bureau of Indian Affairs and spoke out against the state.[231] In this way, "motherhood became a forum to exert political power to disrupt other forms of oppression".[232] But the mother groups also critiqued Indigenous communities and the absence of women leaders. They wrote reports and newspaper articles critiquing the chiefs, but were "careful not to shame Native men".[233] Sarah Nickel notes that "an 1869 Indian Policy statute [in Canada] disallowed Native women to vote in band elections; they could not hold political office, and patrilineality was standardized in defining identity".[234] This created deafness among male Indigenous leaders, but the women in the mother groups pushed back. Again, the women's fight was not for themselves alone, but was first for their families and children, and the betterment of their nations. This is an important contrast to white middle-class feminism that largely centralizes rights for individual women's socioeconomic gain and status.

Statistics and Indigenous organizations for Native women's reproductive health

Forward Together is a national reproductive justice organization that supports all people and communities experiencing reproductive oppression. Their study reported that one out of three Native American respondents in New Mexico had a friend or family member who had an abortion. In addition, the report noted that, of those responding, 20 percent indicated that either they or their partner had received abortion services. The study concludes by declaring that its purpose is to "dispel myths and remind folks of what's real" when it comes to Native Americans and reproductive justice values around body sovereignty and access to reproductive healthcare for all people.[235] The overturning of Roe v. Wade in June 2022 has had a particularly severe impact on Indigenous communities, raising concerns not only about access to medical abortion but also about contraceptive care—areas where Native women already face significant barriers, as "even Plan B pills are rarely available on reservation Indian Health Service centers, which the overturn of Roe exacerbated".[236] Forward Together notes that for Native families to thrive they "must be at the center of building people power…and engaging cultural strategies".[237] A 2020 news article from this organization asserts that Indigenous communities have been at the forefront of fighting for reproductive justice movements and have built significant networks to do so in terms of protesting against federal policy, creating grassroots organizations, and developing community-support programming at all levels of government.[238] One purpose of these assertions is to push back against stereotypes that Native Americans are either not involved in these movements or against access to abortion. On the issue of abortion, a University of Chicago study reports that a "2020 study found that 72% of Native respondents believe that they can hold their own moral views about abortion and still trust a woman and her family to make this decision for themselves…[and] over 80% of Native respondents believe that women and families deserve to make their own healthcare decisions without government interference, including 66% of Native Republicans".[239]

The Native American Women's Health Education Resource Center is a community-focused organization that educates about health issues that specifically impact Indigenous peoples and develops policy agendas for the Indian Health Services and for reproductive justice. They are an international network founded in 1988. The "We Are Here Now" collective serving Indigenous communities in Montana is another key group. They have developed a program called Native Voices, which is an evidence-based sexual health curriculum for American Indian youth that was originally a program called Native Stand designed by the Centers for Disease Control and Prevention. Native Voices, however, centralizes Native cultural knowledges and elder Native mentors focusing on American Indian families and Native youth in their programming and outreach.[240] Carla Knapp, Penobscot Bear Clan and National Vice President of Native Services for the Boys & Girls Clubs of America, proudly notes, "[M]y team and I work with Tribes across the country and each of us hails from different Tribal Nations. Together, we provide the safe spaces, skill-building programs and mentorship that Boys & Girls Clubs offer American Indian, Alaska Native, American Samoan and Native Hawaiian youth".[241] As Indigenous women continue to reclaim their roles as cultural protectors and advocates, their strategies offer valuable lessons for all communities seeking to challenge patriarchal and colonial systems. Recognizing and supporting these efforts is essential to building a future where all people are included and respected.

5
Final thoughts

Discussions about America's historic origins still often begin with when the Pilgrims arrived in North America, as if no sophisticated, technologically advanced civilizations were already flourishing on this soil. Those discussions are then pursued without considering the history of the early Europeans' cultural knowledges and beliefs they brought with them, beyond their questionable goal of securing religious freedom (at least for themselves). The invisible cultural beliefs they carried across the ocean were enacted in very practical ways by those Pilgrims in their everyday lives and tell us about their values concerning gender. Native American people would immediately be affected by those cultural norms. In but a few centuries of their arrival, the colonists' philosophies behind their social norms would be written into the new American constitution, enforced by secular law, and be supported in religious communities under the presumed authority of God. The assumption that Native Americans had similar gender-based beliefs and norms and that they worshipped a single-male deity and functioned under male supremacy are still fallacies rampant in scholarship about Indigenous nations today. Many scholars across various disciplines take the position of "all societies are patriarchal until proven otherwise" instead of "assume nothing about gender until proven what is actually demonstrable and measurable".

Native Americans were catastrophically impacted by colonization at the local, national, and international levels as vastly differing civilizations experiencing invasion at different times and by different means. They strategically and uniquely met those challenges as nations. Participating in Euro-American culture and negotiation with the colonists sometimes allowed some nations to remain more intact and survive better than others, but no nations remained unscathed. The effects of colonization continue in America and Canada today as Native American and First Nations peoples continue to fight for their lives. However, the impact is not equal when we regard the impact of colonization by gender. It is indisputable that all Indigenous peoples across the genders are harmed, but the effect on Indigenous women is profound because of the depth of misogyny culturally embedded in what the Pilgrims brought with them and infected Native people. In addition, Two-Spirited people (LGBTQIA+) are significantly harmed as well because of patriarchal restrictions mandating heterosexual relations and strict expression of gender based on biological sex. The severity of the problem for Indigenous women is captured in this representative statement made to a Euro-American anthropologist in the 1800s—a sentiment echoed in interviews with Indigenous men across the centuries:

> Your laws show how little your men care for their women. The wife is nothing of herself. She is worth little but to help a man...[m]y young men are to lay aside their weapons; they are to take up the work of the women; they will plow the field and raise the crops; for them

> I see a future, but my women, they to whom we owe everything, what is there for them to do? I see nothing![242]

Though the elder quoted was speaking from his era, Indigenous women then, and ever since, saw plenty for themselves and their girls to do to repair the damage of colonization and rebuild the nations. The legacy of colonial patriarchy continues today, as seen in the ongoing battles for reproductive justice, environmental protection, and sovereignty. Organizations like WARN and Forward Together are modern manifestations of the same strategic resilience that Indigenous women have shown for centuries, working tirelessly to reclaim autonomy and protect future generations. As Lakota activist Madonna Thunder Hawk explains, "We are still here, fighting the same battles our grandmothers fought, but with new tools and allies. Our sovereignty starts with our women." Such voices underline the timeless resilience of Indigenous women. The legacy of colonial patriarchy continues to manifest today through barriers to reproductive healthcare, legal battles over Indigenous child welfare, and environmental exploitation that disproportionately impacts Indigenous women. Addressing these issues requires not only acknowledgment but also active resistance and advocacy. Some may argue that efforts to reclaim reproductive sovereignty romanticize precolonial systems or overlook internal community conflicts. However, the evidence presented in this book demonstrates how Indigenous frameworks of Gender Complementarity continue to offer viable models for social, cultural, and political resilience. The stories of resilience shared throughout this book are not simply remnants of a distant past but living testaments to the strength of Indigenous women and communities. Their battles for reproductive justice are intertwined with broader struggles for sovereignty, dignity, and survival. The reclamation of reproductive sovereignty is not only a gendered struggle but one that intersects with racial, cultural, and economic justice. Recognizing these intersections is essential for developing strategies that are inclusive and transformative. The path forward requires a collective commitment to honoring Indigenous knowledge systems, supporting reproductive justice movements, and challenging patriarchal structures that continue to oppress. Readers interested in supporting Indigenous reproductive justice efforts are encouraged to engage with organizations such as WARN, the Native Youth Sexual Health Network, and the Indigenous Women's Network.

For 500 years, Indigenous women have been simultaneously fighting to claim their rightful place within America, and at times even within their own nations, since the settlers arrived. They are ever reimagining and expressing themselves on their own terms, successfully participating in settler society, and governing while being unfailingly traditional Indigenous women in all that means. By doing so, they honor their ancestors and all the struggles that went before them and that still rise up anew on the next horizon. The attacks on their biological reproduction and right to motherhood are but one arena in which Indigenous women must remain vigilant strategists to ensure the protection of their nations and people. Day after day, they are doing it. No matter the historic optics and the research studies claiming otherwise, time and again, Indigenous women are defying 500 years of grave prophecies and state actions meant to undermine and disappear them. As readers, we are called to recognize the enduring strength of Indigenous women and to support their ongoing efforts to reclaim their sovereignty, protect their people, and preserve their traditions. Their indomitable spirit demands more than admiration—it calls for active allyship. Up to this moment and forever, they remain undefeated.

Notes

1. Wagner, *Sisters in Spirit*, 76.
2. Lawrence, "The Indian Health Service," 412.
3. Fox, *Without a Whisper*, 02:36.
4. Christ, "Marija Gimbutas Triumphant."
5. UCLA Costen School, "Event: Marija Gimbutas."
6. Klepp, *Revolutionary Conceptions*, 56.
7. Ibid., 279.
8. Ibid., 56.
9. Grinde and Johansen, "Perceptions of America's Native Democracies," 63.
10. Ibid., 63.
11. Ibid.
12. Ibid., 64.
13. Green, "Native American Women," 265.
14. Seitz, "This Isn't Going to End with Idaho."
15. Steinberg, "JD Vance Thinks Childless Americans."
16. Jefferson, *Notes on the State of Virginia*, 186.
17. Wagner, *Sisters in Spirit*, 88.
18. Grinde and Johansen, "Perceptions of America's Native Democracies," 62–70.
19. Steele, "Thomas Jefferson's Gender Frontier," 17–42.
20. Klepp, *Revolutionary*, 227.
21. Anderson, *A Recognition of Being*, 87.

22. Forbes, "The Urban Tradition," 400.
23. Ibid., 403.
24. Delen and Wright, "Uncovering America's Pyramid."
25. Allen, *Sacred Hoop*, 11.
26. Mann, *Iroquoian Women*, 259.
27. Bartlett, "The Purpose of Women."
28. Cadena, "What's Wrong with Blaming."
29. Wagner, *Sisters in Spirit*, 68, 38.
30. Carey, "Tennessee History."
31. Daly, *Gyn/Ecology*, 227.
32. Ehrenreich and English, *Witches, Midwives*, 87.
33. Joseph et al., "Maternal Mortality in the United States."
34. Moore, "Declared Insane."
35. Pouba and Tianen, "Lunacy in the 19th Century," 96.
36. Saxman, "The Canton Asylum," 41.
37. George, *Mysteries of the Dark Moon*, 35.
38. Safron, Editor's Foreword, x.
39. Isabella, "'Palaeo-Porn.'"
40. Dwass, *Diagnosis Female*, 10.
41. Campbell, *Goddesses*, xx.
42. Mumford, "Woman-Centered," 86.
43. George, *Mysteries of the Dark Moon*, 35.
44. Ibid., 36.
45. Ibid., 37.
46. Ibid.
47. Ibid.
48. Ibid., 38.

49. Ibid.
50. Ehrenreich and English, *Witches, Midwives*, 34.
51. Daly, *Gyn/Ecology*, 196.
52. Ehrenreich and English, *Witches, Midwives*, 40–41.
53. California Mission Trails, see "San Luis Obispo de Tolosa, 5th Mission."
54. LaDuke, "Recovering the Sacred," 303.
55. Mann, *Daughters of Mother Earth*, 96–97.
56. Johnson, *Spider Woman's*, 65.
57. Ibid., 66.
58. Mann, *Iroquoian Women*, 33.
59. Ibid., 33.
60. Ibid., 34.
61. Allen, *Sacred Hoop*, 41.
62. Mann, *Iroquoian Women*, xxiii.
63. Wagner, *Sisters in Spirit*, 30.
64. Ibid., 67.
65. Ibid.
66. Ibid.
67. Smith, *Conquest*, 18.
68. Ibid., 18.
69. Cameron, *Daughters of Copper Woman*, 9.
70. Ibid., 56.
71. Ibid., 44.
72. Todacheene, "She Saves Us," 33.
73. Ibid., 34.
74. Elledge, *Gay, Lesbian, Bisexual*, 15.

75. Ibid., 85.
76. Ibid., 94.
77. Allen, *Sacred Hoop*, 41.
78. Child, *Holding Our World*, 7.
79. Markstrom, *Empowerment of North American*, 107.
80. McGowan, "Weeping for the Lost Matriarchy," 53.
81. Maracle, "Decolonizing Native Women," 32.
82. Markstrom, *Empowerment of North American*, 108.
83. Green, "Native American Women," 266.
84. Klein and Ackerman, *Women and Power*, 243.
85. Grahn, *Blood, Bread, and Roses*, 9.
86. Moulton, "Venus Envy."
87. Allen, *Sacred Hoop*, 14.
88. Ibid., 32.
89. Denetdale, "Chairmen, Presidents," 10.
90. Mann, *Iroquoian Women*, 259.
91. Child, *Holding Our World*, 7–8.
92. Native American Women's Health Resource Center.
93. Grandey et al., "Tackling Taboo Topics," 8.
94. George, *Mysteries of the Dark Moon*, 203.
95. Ibid., 202.
96. Ibid., 208–209.
97. Ibid., 212.
98. Ibid.
99. Ibid., 215.
100. Wagner, *Sisters in Spirit*, 10.
101. Child, *Holding Our World*, 4–5.

102. Ibid., 5.
103. Ibid., 6.
104. Ibid., 5.
105. Ibid.
106. Ibid., 7.
107. Ibid.
108. Ibid., 8.
109. Carr, *Kinaalda*.
110. Markstrom, *Empowerment of North American*, 338.
111. Ibid., 325.
112. Crow Dog, *Lakota Woman*, 246.
113. Ibid., 246–247.
114. Ibid., 67.
115. Ibid.
116. Allen, *Sacred Hoop*, 47.
117. Ibid., 47.
118. Gurr, "Mothering in the Borderlands," 71.
119. Ibid., 71.
120. Mann, *Iroquoian Women*, 254.
121. Wagner, *Sisters in Spirit*, 47.
122. Driskill et al., *Queer Indigenous Studies*, 109.
123. Mann, *Iroquoian Women*, 260–261.
124. Ibid., 259.
125. Jefferson, *Notes on the State of Virginia*, 186.
126. Lawrence, "The Indian Health Service," 412.
127. Mann, *Iroquoian Women*, 261–262.
128. Anderson, *A Recognition of Being*, 88.

129. Hoffert, "Childbearing on the Trans-Mississippi Frontier," 285.
130. Jefferson, *Notes on the State of Virginia*, 262.
131. Mann, *Iroquoian Women*, 266.
132. Cooper, "Childbirth in Colonial America."
133. Klepp, *Revolutionary Conceptions*, 4.
134. Mann, *Iroquoian Women*, 259.
135. Ibid., 267.
136. Ibid., 262.
137. Ibid.
138. Child, *Holding Our World*, 16.
139. Smith, *Conquest*, 70.
140. Native American Women's Health Education Resource Center.
141. Konsmo, "Native History."
142. Devens, "If We Get the Girls," 285.
143. Smith, *Conquest*, 8.
144. Mann, *Iroquoian Women*, 6.
145. Lajimodiere, "Ogimah Ikwe," 57.
146. Child, *Holding Our World*, 63.
147. Pink et al., "Rationale, Design, and Methods," 2.
148. van Schilfgaarde, "Native Reproductive Justice."
149. Gurr, "Mothering in the Borderlands," 72.
150. Ibid., 71.
151. Allen, *Sacred Hoop*, 41–42.
152. Ibid., 39.
153. Ibid., 37.
154. Ibid., 38.

155. Bruyneel, "Race, Colonialism," 4.
156. Devens, "If We Get the Girls," 286.
157. Ibid., 285.
158. Ibid., 284.
159. Ibid., 289.
160. Crow Dog, *Lakota Woman*, 32–33.
161. Ibid., 33.
162. Ibid., 35.
163. Lawrence, "The Indian Health Service," 410.
164. Ibid., 400.
165. Ibid.
166. Ibid., 411
167. Ibid., 406.
168. Ibid.
169. Ibid.
170. Ibid.
171. Ibid., 411.
172. Dwyer-Lindgren, "Ten Americas."
173. Gurr, "Mothering in the Borderlands," 74.
174. Loerzel, "Policy, Wellness."
175. Smith, *Conquest*, 10.
176. Ibid., 15.
177. Ibid., 107.
178. LaDuke, "Indigenous Environmental Perspectives," 380.
179. Smith, *Conquest*, 67.
180. Ibid., 67.
181. Ibid., 66.

182. Ibid., 67.
183. WARN, "Radiation," 22.
184. Lame Deer, "Alone on the Hilltop," 304.
185. Crow Dog, *Lakota Woman*, 29.
186. Fawcett, *Medicine Trail*, 114.
187. Ibid., 115.
188. Ibid., 34.
189. National Indian Child Welfare Association.
190. Torpy, "Native American Women," 175.
191. Ibid., 176.
192. Ibid.
193. Ibid.
194. Congressional Research Service.
195. Ibid., 177.
196. Ibid.
197. Ibid.
198. Wikipedia, "Indian Child Welfare Act."
199. Native American Rights Fund, "Indian Child Welfare Act."
200. Pevar, "In South Dakota."
201. Fox et al., "American Indian Female Leadership," 84–85.
202. Ibid., 87.
203. Ibid., 82.
204. Lajimodiere, "Ogimah Ikwe," 70.
205. Mankiller, "Rebuilding the Cherokee."
206. Lajimodiere, "Ogimah Ikwe," 70.
207. Ibid., 71.
208. Lipschutz, *Young Lakota*, 17:39–44.

209. Mann, *Iroquoian Women*, 262–263.

210. Ibid., 264.

211. Ibid.

212. Crow Dog, *Lakota Woman*, 3.

213. Child, *Holding Our World*, xxvi.

214. Lipschutz, *Young Lakota*, 13:12–21.

215. Green, "Native American Women," 266.

216. Tohe, "There Is No Word," 103.

217. Ibid.

218. Ibid., 104.

219. Nickel, "I'm Not a Women's Libber," 301.

220. Ibid.

221. Smith, "Native American Feminism," 121.

222. Ibid., 118.

223. Lajimodiere, "Ogimah Ikwe," 63.

224. Ibid., 64.

225. Fawcett, *Medicine Trail*, 15.

226. Ibid., 15.

227. Ibid., 53.

228. Ibid.

229. Ibid., 55.

230. "Women Are Sacred."

231. Nickel, "I'm Not a Women's Libber," 305.

232. Ibid., 308.

233. Ibid., 314.

234. Ibid., 309.

235. Lajimodiere, "Ogimah Ikwe," 5.

236. Planned Parenthood, "Indigenous Health Rights."
237. Forward Together, "The Road to Reproductive Justice," 1.
238. Ibid., 1.
239. BlackDeer, "Towards an Indigenous Reproductive Justice," 2.
240. Green, "Native American Women," 9.
241. Knapp, Carla.
242. Wagner, *Sisters in Spirit*, 76.

Recommended projects & discussion questions

- Who are the female deities in your cultural or religious traditions? Research your ancestral origins and find images of them. What messages do they convey about the roles of women in society? In relation to men?
- Research a few Native American women leaders from the nineteenth century and create a PowerPoint presentation. What were their primary objectives for their people?
- Research Native American women leaders elected to tribal offices today. What platforms did they run on and how prominent was female reproduction?
- Identify the impacts of the enforcement of heteropatriarchal values in Native American communities. How was it accomplished by the U.S. government and its allies?
- What are the steps to healing the sacred hoop of Indigenous life in the United States? How are those strategies in place in Native nations today?

Bibliography

Allen, Paula Gunn. Foreword to *Iroquoian Women: The Gantowisas*, by Barbara Alice Mann. Peter Lang, 2004, ix–xxv.

———. *The Sacred Hoop*. Beacon Press, 1986.

Anderson, Kim. *A Recognition of Being: Reconstructing Native Womanhood*. Sumach Press, 2000.

Bartlett, Beth. "The Purpose of Women," Feminism and Religion Blog. September 21, 2024. https://feminismandreligion.com/2024/09/21/the-purpose-of-women-by-beth-bartlett/. Accessed October 7, 2024.

BlackDeer, Autumn Asher. "Towards an Indigenous Reproductive Justice: Examining Attitudes on Abortion among American Indian and Alaska Native Communities," NORC at the University of Chicago Blog. May 2023. https://www.norc.org/content/dam/norc-org/pdfs/NORC%20Research%20Brief_AABreprojustice_FINAL.pdf. Accessed November 18, 2024.

Bruyneel, Kevin. "Race, Colonialism, and the Politics of Indian Sports Names and Mascots: The Washington Football Team Case." *Native American and Indigenous Studies*, Vol 3, Issue 2, Fall 2016.

Cadena, Denicia and Micaela Cadena. "What's Wrong with Blaming Teen Parents?," American Civil Liberties Union Blog. August 24, 2012. https://www.aclu.org/news/womens-rights/whats-wrong-blaming-teen-parents#:~:text=The%20negative%20practice%20of%20shaming,United%20States%20%248.63%20billion%20annually. Accessed September 4, 2024.

"California Mission Trails." California State Parks Website. https://www.parks.ca.gov/?page_id=22722. Accessed October 7, 2024.

Carey, Bill. "Tennessee History: Newspaper 'Ads' for Runaway Wives Were Once Common," *Williamson Herald*, August 5, 2020. https://www.williamsonherald.com/opinion/tennessee-history-newspaper-ads-for-runaway-wives-were-once-common/article_a677e594-d78a-11ea-aa38-2704f1fe6f78.html. Accessed October 7, 2024.

Carr, Lena, dir. *Kinaalda: Navajo Rite of Passage*. VisionMaker Media, 2000.

Child, Brenda J. *Holding Our World Together: Ojibwe Women and the Survival of Community*. Viking Penguin, 2012.

Christ, Carol, "Marija Gimbutas Triumphant: Colin Renfrew Concedes," December 11, 2017. https://feminismandreligion.com/2017/12/11/marija-gimbutas-triumphant-colin-renfrew-concedes-by-carol-p-christ/. Accessed April 24, 2024.

Congressional Research Service. "Child Welfare: Purposes, Federal Programs, and Funding," February 23, 2024. https://crsreports.congress.gov/product/pdf/IF/IF10590/41#:~:text=Under%20IV%2DE%2C%20states%20d,this%20share%20varies%20by%20state. Accessed November 11, 2024.

Cooper, Elaine Marie. "Childbirth in Colonial America," Heroes, Heroines, and History Blog. August 29, 2019. https://www.hhhistory.com/2019/08/childbirth-in-colonial-america.html. Accessed October 19, 2024.

Crow Dog, Mary. *Lakota Woman*. HarperPerennial, 1991.

Daly, Mary. *Gyn/Ecology: The Metaethics of Radical Feminism*. Beacon, 1978.

Delen, Grant and Karen Wright. "Uncovering America's Pyramid Builders: The Grandest Culture North of the Maya Created a City of 20,000 People, Built Pyramids Reviling Egypt's Great Pyramid, Then Vanished into Oblivion," *Discover Magazine*, February 4, 2004. https://www.discovermagazine.com/the-sciences/uncovering-americas-pyramid-builders. Accessed December 2, 2024.

Devens, Carol. "If We Get the Girls, We Get the Race," in *Native American Voices: A Reader*, 3rd edition, Susan Lobo et al., eds. Routledge, 2010.

Driskill, Qwo-Li, Chris Finley, Brian Joseph Gilley, and Scott Lauria Morgensen, eds. *Queer Indigenous Studies: Critical Interventions in Theory, Politics, and Literature*. University of Arizona Press, 2011.

Dwass, Emily. *Diagnosis Female: How Medical Bias Endangers Women's Health*. Rowman & Littlefield, 2019.

Dwyer-Lindgren, Laura, Mathew M. Baumann, Zhuochen Li, Yekaterina O. Kelly, Chris Schmidt, Chloe Searchinger, et al. "Ten Americas: A Systemic Analysis of Life Expectancy Disparities in the USA," *The Lancet*, November 21, 2024. https://www.thelancet.com/journals/lancet/article/PIIS0140-6736(24)01495-8/fulltext. Accessed December 2, 2024

Ehrenreich, Barbara and Deirdre English, eds. *Witches, Midwives, and Nurses: A History of Women Healers*. The Feminist Press at CUNY, 2010.

Elledge, Jim, ed. *Gay, Lesbian, Bisexual and Transgender Myths: From the Arapaho to the Zuni*. Peter Lang, 2002.

Fawcett, Melissa Jayne. *Medicine Trail: The Life and Lessons of Gladys Tantaquidgeon*. University of Arizona Press, 2000.

Forbes, Jack. "The Urban Tradition among Native Americans," in *Native American Voices: A Reader*, 3rd edition. Susan Lobo et al., eds. Routledge, 2010.

Forward Together. "The Road to Reproductive Justice: Native Americans in New Mexico," 2020 Report. https://forwardtogether.org/programs/state-national-action/strongfamiliesnm/. Accessed November 18, 2024.

Fox, Katsitsionni, Director. *Without a Whisper—Konnon:Kwe*, Women Make Movies, 2020.

Fox, Mary Jo Tippeconnic, Eileen M. Luna-Firebaugh, and Caroline Williams. "American Indian Female Leadership," *Wicazo Sa Review* (Spring 2015).

George, Demetra. *Mysteries of the Dark Moon: The Healing Power of the Dark Goddess*. HarperOne, 1992.

Grahn, Judy. *Blood, Bread, and Roses: How Menstruation Created the World*. Beacon Press, 1993.

Grandey, Alicia A., Allison S. Gabriel, and Eden B. King. "Tackling Taboo Topics: A Review of the Three Ms in Working Women's Lives," *Journal of Management*, 46, 1 (2020), 7–35.

Green, Rayna. "Native American Women," *Signs*, 6, 2 (1980). http://www.jstor.org/stable/3173925. Accessed October 16, 2024.

Grinde, Jr., Donald A. and Bruce E. Johansen. "Perceptions of America's Native Democracies," in *Native American Voices: A Reader,* 3rd edition. Susan Lobo et al., eds. Routledge, 2010.

Gurr, Barbara. "Mothering in the Borderlands: Policing Native American Women's Reproductive Healthcare," *International Journal of Sociology of the Family*, 37, 1 (Spring 2011).

Hoffert, Sylvia D. "Childbearing on the Trans-Mississippi Frontier, 1830–1900," *Western Historical Quarterly*, 22, 3 (1991).

Isabella, Jude. "'Palaeo-Porn': We've Got It All Wrong," *New Scientist* Blog, November 7, 2012. https://www.newscientist.com/article/mg21628900-300-palaeo-porn-weve-got-it-all-wrong/. Accessed December 13, 2024.

Jefferson, Thomas. *Writings: Autobiography, A Summary View of the Rights of British America, Notes on the State of Virginia, Public Papers, Addresses, Messages, and Replies, Miscellany, Letters*. The Library of America, 1984.

Johnson, E. Pauline. "The Woman Who Fell from the Sky," in *Spider Woman's Granddaughters: Traditional Tales and Contemporary*

Writing by Native American Women, Paula Gunn Allen, ed. Fawcett Columbine, 1989.

Joseph, K. S., et al. "Maternal Mortality in the United States: Are the High and Rising Rates Due to Changes in Obstetrical Factors, Maternal Medical Conditions, or Maternal Mortality Surveillance?," *American Journal of Obstetrics & Gynecology*, 230, 4. https://www.ajog.org/article/S0002-9378(24)00005- X/fulltext#:~:text=Despite%20these%20changes%20in%20surveillance,100%2C000%20liv e%20births%20in%202021. Accessed January 6, 2025.

Klepp, Susan E. *Revolutionary Conceptions: Women, Fertility, & Family Limitation in America, 1760–1820*. University of North Carolina Press, 2009.

Knapp, Carla. Boys & Girls Club of America. October 17, 2024. https://www.bgca.org/news-stories/2024/October/what-native-youth-want-us-to-know/. Accessed February 17, 2025.

LaDuke, Winona. "Indigenous Environmental Perspectives: A North American Primer," in *Native American Voices: A Reader*, 3rd edition. Susan Lobo et al., eds. Routledge, 2010.

———. "Recovering the Sacred Power of Naming and Claiming," in *Native American Voices: A Reader*, 3rd edition. Susan Lobo et al., eds. Routledge, 2010.

Lajimodiere, Denise K. "Ogimah Ikwe: Native Women and Their Path to Leadership," *Wicazo Sa Review* (Fall 2011).

Lame Deer, John (Fire) and Richard Erdoes. "Alone on the Hilltop," in *Native American Voices: A Reader*, 3rd edition, Susan Lobo et al., eds. Prentice Hall, 2010.

Lipschutz, Mario and Rose Rosenblatt, directors. *Young Lakota*. Cine Qua Non, United States, 2013. Film.

Loerzel, Em. "Policy, Wellness, and Native American Survivorship," Medicine and Society section, *AMA Journal of Ethics*, October

2020. https://journalofethics.ama-assn.org/article/policy-wellness-and-native-american- survivorship/2020-10#:~:text=9,abuse%20to%20the%20federal%20government. Accessed November 4, 2024.

Mankiller, Wilma. "Rebuilding the Cherokee Nation—April 2, 1993," Iowa State University Speech. Archives of Women's Political Communication. https://awpc.cattcenter.iastate.edu/2017/03/21/rebuilding-the-cherokee-nation-april-2-1993/. Accessed November 11, 2024.

Mann, Barbara Alice. *Daughters of Mother Earth: The Wisdom of Native American Women*. Praeger, 2006.

———. *George Washington's War on Native America*. University of Nebraska Press, 2008.

———. *Iroquoian Women: The Gantowisas*. Peter Lang, 2004.

Maracle, Lee. "Decolonizing Native Women," in *Daughters of Mother Earth: The Wisdom of Native American Women*, Barbara Alice Mann, ed. Praeger, 2006.

Markstrom, Carol A. *Empowerment of North American Indian Girls: Ritual Expressions at Puberty*. University of Nebraska Press, 2008.

McGowan, Kay Givens. "Weeping for the Lost Matriarchy," in *Daughters of Mother Earth: The Wisdom of Native American Women*, Barbara Alice Mann, ed. Praeger, 2006.

Monkman, Kent. "The Scream," 2017. Art Canada Institute. https://www.aci-iac.ca/art-books/kent-monkman/key-works/the-scream/. Accessed November 11, 2024.

Moore, Kate. "Declared Insane for Speaking Up: The Dark American History of Silencing Women Through Psychiatry," *Time Magazine*. June 22, 2021. https://time.com/6074783/psychiatry- history-women-mental-health/. Accessed September 6, 2024.

Moulton, Susan. "Venus Envy: A Sexual Epistemology," *ReVision*, 21, 3 (1999). *Gale Academic OneFile*. https://link.gale.com/apps/doc/A53963818/AONE?u= anon~6b569ffd&sid=googleScholar&xid=6ac1f104. Accessed September 20, 2024.

Mumford, Marilyn R. "Woman-Centered Myth in Anne Cameron's *Daughters of Copper Woman* and Dzelarhons," *CEA Critic*, 50, 1 (1987), 84–91. http://www.jstor.org/stable/44377015. Accessed September 25, 2024.

Native American Rights Fund. "Indian Child Welfare Act (ICWA) Haaland v. Brackeen," June 2023. https://narf.org/cases/brackeen-v-bernhardt/. Accessed November 8, 2024.

Native American Women's Health Education Resource Center. "Reproductive Justice Programs," https://www.nativeshop.org/. Accessed November 19, 2024.

National Indian Child Welfare Association. "About ICWA," https://www.nicwa.org/about-icwa/. Accessed November 8, 2024.

Nickel, Sarah A. "I'm Not a Women's Libber—Although Sometimes I Sound Like One: Indigenous Feminism and Politicized Motherhood," *American Indian Quarterly*, 41, 4 (Fall 2017).

Pevar, Stephen. "In South Dakota, Officials Defied a Federal Judge and Took Indian Kids Away from Their Parents in Rigged Proceedings," American Civil Liberties Union Blog, February 22, 2017. https://www.aclu.org/news/racial-justice/south-dakota-officials-defied-federal-judge-and-took#:~:text=It's%20worth%20noting%20that%20in,2012)%2C%20is%20available%20here. Accessed November 8, 2024.

Planned Parenthood of Greater New York. "Indigenous Health Rights Are Reproductive Justice," November 22, 2023. https://www.plannedparenthood.org/planned-parenthood-greater-new-york/blog/indigenous-health-rights-are-reproductive-justice-2#:~:text=As%20a%20leading%20organization%20for,to%20receive%20care%20at%20PP GNY. Accessed November 18, 2024.

Pouba, Katherine and Ashley Tianen. "Lunacy in the 19th Century: Women's Admission to Asylums in the United States of America," *Oshkosh Scholar*, 1 (April 2006), 95–103.

Rink, Elizabeth, Paula Firemoon, Michael Anastario, Olivia Johnson, Ramey Growing Thunder, Adriann Ricker, Malory Peterson, and Julie Baldwin. "Rationale, Design and Methods for Nen Unkumbi/Edahiyedo ('We Are Here Now'): A Multi-Level Randomized Controlled Trial to Improve Sexual and Reproductive Health Outcomes in a Northern Plains American Indian Reservation Community," *Frontiers in Public Health*, 10, 823228 (July 13, 2022).

Rose, Christina. "Native History: Roe v. Wade Passes, But Indian Women Lack Access," *Indian Country Today*, January 22, 2014. https://ictnews.org/archive/native-history-roe-v-wade-passes-but-indigenous-women-lack-access. Accessed June 12, 2016.

Safron, Rossi, Editor's Foreword in *Goddesses: Mysteries of the Feminine Divine*, by Joseph Campbell. New World Library, 2013.

Saxman, Michelle C. "The Canton Asylum for Insane Indians," *Cultural Resource Management*, 22, 9 (1999), 41. Accessed September 25, 2024. https://www.nps.gov/crps/CRMJournal/CRM/v22n9.pdf.

Seitz, Amanda. "This Isn't Going to End with Idaho," Associated Press. April 24, 2024. https://apnews.com/live/supreme-court-abortion-idaho. Accessed May 1, 2024.

Smith, Andrea. *Conquest: Sexual Violence and American Indian Genocide*. South End Press, 2005.

———. "Native American Feminism, Sovereignty, and Social Change," *Feminist Studies*, 31,1 (Spring 2005).

Steele, Brian. "Thomas Jefferson's Gender Frontier," *Journal of American History*, 95, 1 (June 2008).

Steinberg, Neil. "JD Vance Thinks Childless Americans Have No Stake in Society. He's Wrong," *Chicago Sun-Times*. July 25, 2024. https://chicago.suntimes.com/columnists/2024/07/25/parenthood-children-jd-vance-kamala-harris-politics-families-2024- presidential-election. Accessed September 2, 2024.

Todacheene, Heidi J. "She Saves Us from Monsters: The Navajo Creation Story and Modern Tribal Justice," *Tribal Law Journal* 15, 1 (2014). https://digitalrepository.unm.edu/cgi/viewcontent.cgi? article=1071&context=tlj. Accessed September 28, 2024.

Tohe, Laura. "There Is No Word for Feminism in My Language," *Wicazo Sa Review*, 15, 2 (Fall 2000).

Torpy, Sally J. "Native American Women and Coerced Sterilization on the Trails of Tears in the 1970s," in *Native American Voices*, Susan Lobo et al., eds. Routledge, 2010.

UCLA Costen School of Archaeology Round Table Panel. "Event: Marija Gimbutas: A Magnificent Vindication," https://ioa.ucla.edu/content/marija-gimbutas-magnificent-vindication. Accessed April 24, 2024.

van Schilfgaarde, Lauren. "Native Reproductive Justice: Practices and Policies from Relinquishment to Family Preservation," Harvard Law Blog, May 12, 2022. https://blog.petrieflom.law.harvard.edu/2022/05/12/native-reproductive-justice-adoption- relinquishment-family-preservation/. Accessed November 18, 2024.

Wagner, Sally Roesch. *Sisters in Spirit: Haudenosaunee (Iroquois) Influence on Early American Feminists*. Native Voices, 2001.

Wikipedia. "Indian Child Welfare Act," https://en.wikipedia.org/wiki/Indian_Child_Welfare_Act. Accessed November 8, 2024.

Women Are Sacred Conference. https://www.niwrc.org/women-are-sacred. Accessed February 17, 2025.

Women of All Red Nations. "Radiation: Dangerous to Pine Ridge Women," *Akwesasne Notes* (Early Spring 1980).

About the author

Dr Stephanie A. Sellers holds a Ph.D. in Native American Studies specializing in Women of the Eastern Woodlands. Her doctoral work was mentored by Paula Gunn Allen and Barbara Alice Mann. Sellers developed and currently teaches many courses in Native American Studies at Gettysburg College where she has been a professor since 2000. Her highly popular course "Native American Women" was the springboard for her 2008 book titled *Native American Women's Studies: A Primer* (Peter Lang). Sellers is also a poet and since 2017 has annually contributed to the We'Moon Datebook of Writing and Art by Womyn. In 2023, her book addressing global anti-female family violence, titled *Daughters Healing from Family Mobbing*, was published by North Atlantic Books and is distributed globally by Penguin Random House. Sellers, with lots of help from her Welshmen (husband and corgi), cultivates a cottage garden on her homestead in Pennsylvania that is filled with antique daffodils and medicinal plants.

Index

"We Are Here Now" Collective of Montana 122

Abortifacients 78, 107

Abortion 9, 10, 25, 59, 76, 78, 79, 80, 83, 84, 87, 99, 106, 107, 121, 140

Adam and Eve 21

Allen, Paula Gunn 19, 48, 49, 70, 86, 112, 140, 144, 149

American Gynecology 24

American Indian Movement 94

Apess, William 42

Aquinas, Thomas 22

Articles of Confederation 11

Beloved Woman xi, 52, 87, 114

Berry Fast 60, 65, 66, 67, 68, 70

Birth Control 10, 12, 59, 75, 76, 78, 79, 80, 94, 95, 96

Brigadier General James Clinton 42

Caesarean sections 25

Campbell, Joseph 27, 29, 147

Carr, Lucien 19

Changing Woman 44, 46, 67, 86, 115

Chief Cecelia Fire Thunder 106, 111

Chief Wilma Mankiller 13, 106

Child, Brenda J. 57, 65, 66, 111, 132, 134, 137, 141

Colden, Cadwallader 6, 10, 54

Coming-of-Age Ceremony vii, 48, 57, 59, 67, 68, 69, 90

Concealment, crime of 13

Cook, Katsi v, 99

Copper Woman 42, 43, 44, 46, 69, 86, 131, 146

Corporate Feminism 105, 115

Covington, Lucy xiii, 49

Crow Dog, Leonard 70

Crow Dog, Mary 91, 100, 108, 141

Dawes Act 87, 88

Denetdale, Jennifer 48, 53, 132

Divine Creatrix vii, xv, 16, 19, 27, 29, 36, 38, 43, 44, 46, 49, 50, 52, 53, 61, 67, 86, 89

Driskill, Qwo-Li 45, 46, 75, 142

Dwass, Emily 28, 130, 142

Environmental Impacts 85, 98, 125

European Women's Holocaust 31

Extractive Industries 85, 96, 98

Fielding, Emma Tyler 118
First Nations of British Columbia's Indian Homemakers' Club 118
Forward Together 120, 121, 125, 138, 142
Freud, Sigmund 25

Gantowisas 82, 140, 145
Gender Binary 34, 35
Gender Complementary social structure vii, 16, 17, 33, 35, 37, 40, 42, 58, 60
Gender Fluidity 21, 41, 45, 73, 74
General Allotment Act 87, 88
Gimbutas, Marija 2, 27, 129, 141, 148
Goddess Cultures 2, 26, 27, 29
Green, Rayna 7, 49, 112, 143
Gurr, Barbara 84, 133, 134, 135, 143

Handsom Lake 107
Hangings 74
Herne, Louise v
Hiawatha Insane Asylum for Indians 26

Indian Boarding School xii, 81, 85, 87, 88, 89, 90, 92, 93, 97, 100, 102, 107, 112
Indian Child Welfare Act 102, 136, 146, 148
Indian Health Services 83, 122

Indigenous Feminisms 54, 113, 114, 116
Indigenous Women's Network 119, 126
Ishna Ta Awi Cha Lowan 60, 68

Jefferson, Thomas 9, 76, 129, 143, 147
John (Fire) Lame Deer 99
Joseph-Francois Lafitau 75
Judge Sir William Blackstone 23

Kanati 46
Kinaalda 60, 67, 68, 141

Lauren van Schilfgaarde 83

Madonna Thunder Hawk 125
Mann, Barbara 38, 48, 57, 71, 76, 78, 107, 140, 145, 149
Mann, Henrietta 36
Maracle, Lee 48, 132, 145
Matriarchies 47, 48
Matrilineage 4, 11, 30, 38, 40, 44, 59, 91, 115
McKeag, Jana x
Menarche 58, 59, 60, 61, 62, 63, 65, 68, 70, 88, 91, 92
Menstrual Rites 30, 61, 62
Mindimooyenh 82
Missing and Murdered Indigenous Women and Girls 96, 108

Index 153

Mitchell, Ceceilia 78
Mohegan Nation's Church Ladies Sewing Society 118
Monkman, Kent 101, 145
Mormon Church 101, 102
Mother Goddess 2, 26, 27, 28, 29, 32, 36, 37, 50, 62
Mother-Daughter Bond 44, 71

Native American Women's Health Resource Center 59, 132
Native Services for the Boys & Girls Clubs of America 122
Native Voices Program 122
Native Youth Sexual Health Network 79, 80, 108, 126
Nokomis 46, 69

Ogimah Ikwe 82, 134, 136, 137, 144

Paleo Porn 28
Paradise Myth 21, 24, 31
Parker, Arthur 77
Penis Envy 25
Penn, William 3
Pilgrims 26, 30, 31, 32, 123, 124
Primogeniture 22, 23, 30, 72

Roosevelt, Teddy 88
Runaway Wife Ads 141

Sagard, Gabriel 75
Selu 46
Sky Woman 37, 38, 39, 40, 44, 46, 52, 69, 86
Smith, Andrea 78, 81, 97, 98, 117, 131, 134, 135, 137, 147
Sterilization 82, 85, 93, 94, 95, 107, 148

Tantaquidgeon, Gladys 100, 142
The Malleus Maleficarum 31
Trimble, Chuck xiii
Two-Spirits 93

U.S. Bureau of Indian Affairs 89

Venus Envy 52, 132, 146
Virgin-Whore Metaphor 72, 75

Wade, Roe v. 8, 121, 147
Wagner, Sally Roesch 115, 129, 130, 131, 132, 133, 138, 148
Waiting House 43, 60
Washington, George 11, 145
White Buffalo Calf Woman 46, 47, 69
Witchcraze 30, 31
Women of All Red Nations 99, 119, 148

Zitkala-Sa 90

www.ingramcontent.com/pod-product-compliance
Lightning Source LLC
Chambersburg PA
CBHW070807230426
43665CB00017B/2524